**What Tom's readers say al
responses:**

Maria: "Why is it that middle-aged geezers want to date 20 year-olds? There are many very attractive, sexually active, women in their 50s and beyond." Response: *Last night I went out with someone only 19 years younger, so I'm making progress.*

Janet: "I've been married four times. I appreciate your courage. You just open your stomach and let your guts fall out for all of the world to see." Response: *Four marriages? That's scary.*

Loretta: "I give you a lot of credit--you give us hope. You're very good looking for your age." Response: *Why did you have to add, "for your age?"*

Judy: "I was surprised and impressed to learn that you can cry." Response: *A person who can cry has the capability to be deeply touched.*

Norma: "You got what you deserved taking out that younger woman. At 50 cents a minute, she undercharged you because obviously she was bored stiff. Maybe she feels ripped off." Response: *How could she? She had a double helping of calamari.*

Micholena: "Good grief, get a life. You're wimping along, far too long...your whining will only attract flies." Response: *Now I understand what 'cutting to the quick' means. You've got a bee in your butt.*

Diane: "You've opened my eyes to the guy's side of middle aged dating." Response: *Experience teaches us well.*

# Middle Aged

## and

# Dating Again

# TOM BLAKE

**Published by**
**Tooter's Publishing, Dana Point, California**

Copyright © 1997
Thomas P. Blake

Published by Tooter's Publishing
Dana Point, California

Library of Congress Catalog Card Number: 97-92964
ISBN 1-57502-423-3

Additional copies may be obtained by sending a check for $15.45 (includes postage) to the address below. For your convenience, an order form can be found at the back of this book

Middle Aged and Dating Again
15 Reina
Dana Point, CA 92629

Printed in the USA by

Morris
PUBLISHING

3212 E. Hwy 30
Kearney, NE 68847
800-650-7888

# I dedicate this collection to:

My mom, Fran, the most sensible woman in the world

Brother, Bill, and his wife, Linda

Sisters, Pam and Chris, and Captain Pete

Nephews, Derek and Rod

Deli customers, friends, and column readers

The single women of Orange County, California, who
provided most of the information upon which the book
is based

*The Orange County Register* employees, Sherrie Good and
Dixie Redfearn, my first editors, who gave me the chance

Johnny Cash, and his manager, Lou Robin, for years
of friendship

Teresa and Rosa, for being there daily, for nine years

The Jay-Bird and Kanan, for entering my life, and for
tolerating my endless hours in my office, while
preparing this book

Kira, whose loyalty never wavered

# TABLE OF CONTENTS

# INTRODUCTION

Most of us middle-aged people thought that by the time we reached age 55, we would be taking life easy. Our kids would be married, and living productive lives. Grandchildren would be a pleasure and a happy retirement nearing. With our mortgages paid off, we could settle back and enjoy a life of leisure. Tee up the golf ball every day. Lunch at the country club, dinner out a few times a month. The old pension would soon be kicking in. It would be a time to travel, to see the world. We'd put our feet up and enjoy the rewards of all those years of hard work. Three years ago, I had all of that.

Then, my life took an unexpected turn. I was dealt a new set of cards. My wife left me. I won't bore you with why. Dreams of retirement vanished. I had to continue working to pay the mortgage. My savings were depleted. I was alone, lonely, and confused. I wanted to find a partner so I could start rebuilding my life. I entered the dating world. It's a jungle.

Based upon my dating experiences, I started to write a newspaper column entitled, "Middle Aged and Dating." *The Orange County Register*, in Orange County, California, owns a group of newspapers called *The Register Community Newspapers.* Seven of those papers feature my column.

This column has developed a following because so many people are in the same situation as I--middle aged, alone, trying to make ends meet, and trying to find a mate. Column subjects include blind dates, dating people who are younger or older, who pays on dates, getting dumped, two-stepping, back-stepping and eating tons of pasta at a myriad of Italian restaurants. I've dated widows, spinsters and divorcees. I've had bad luck, some luck and no luck.

**This book is a collection of the first 50 newspaper columns, each slightly rewritten.**

At the end of each column is a comments section for readers. In there, I get bashed, bruised, criticized, and sometimes complimented. One reader called me, "a gemstone in a pile of rocks," while another, "a sniveling puke." She still asked me out. A blue-eyed blonde from Santa Barbara, said, "I'm amused, the only reason you're writing the column is to fill up a pile of black address books." She didn't help, she failed to leave her name and number.

The *purpose* of this book is to give support and encouragement to "middle aged and dating" folks, to let them know they aren't alone, and that the frustrations they're finding are the same ones being faced all over the world. It's a large fraternity, there are millions of us. The size of our group is growing by leaps and bounds. Nearly every week, one hears of another divorce war story. "John left Susie after 27 years of marriage to run off with a 23-year-old topless dancer." By reading this book, perhaps a little insight will be gained about middle aged dating.

Another *purpose* is to make us **laugh** because if we can't laugh at what's happening to us, we're in deep poop.

This book is unique because it's based on a man's personal dating experiences. It wasn't written in the ivory towers of some college campus. I don't hold a Phd in middle aged dating. This book was written by a regular guy who owns a delicatessen, who struggles to make ends meet and who's spent more time with his face down in the dating trenches than most normal folks spend in church in a lifetime.

I'm middle aged--57 years old. I've been married and divorced three times. Marriages lasted 4 years, 4 years, and 6 years. I've been through the dating ringer more than I've been married.

My buddy, Wams, of Mill Valley, California, recently said to me, "Two things we shouldn't have to be doing at our age is earning a living, and trying to dork the world." Now, I'm trying to do both.

Oh, it's just a coincidence that the title, "Middle Aged and Dating Again," is an acronynm for **"Mad Again"**. Have a fun read. I hope you enjoy it as much as I enjoyed the experiences upon which the book is based.

## Column 1

# LIVING ALONE WITH ONLY MY DOGS FOR COMPANY

It's unfortunate, but many of us have been there, are there now, or will be there soon. Where? Dating again after our marriage has ended.

I won't bore you with why my wife and I separated. I will tell you the separation occurred on Christmas Eve., 1993, while I was visiting my 83 year-old mother.

My wife backed up a U-haul truck to the front door of our home, took what furniture and belongings she wanted, and moved away. She never told me she planned to do this. I was clueless.

Christmas was not Merry for me at age 54. It's strange how holidays have a funny way of testing relationships.

Up until then, I thought she and I would soon be heading for the retirement golf life. I never dreamed I would be alone, starting over at my age. I felt I was too together of a person for this to ever happen to me. Sometimes God makes relationship-ending decisions for us. In our case, my wife made the decision.

Enough of the family history. These columns won't look back, except for an occasional point of clarification or poison dart. Besides, there are two sides to every divorce.

# MIDDLE AGED AND DATING AGAIN

These columns will focus on what happens **after the separation.** I know my topic. I'm living it, trying to find my way "out there" in the middle-aged singles world. It's a jungle.

It's the night after Christmas. I return home. My wife informed me by phone at my mom's place that she had left. I don't know what to expect when I enter the house. As the garage door opens, my dogs bark. They're still here. Nothing else really matters. I'm alone for the first time in 8 years. Later, my dogs are in the kitchen with me, tilting their heads, confused because I'm crying.

The house is pretty empty. Marital asset-division isn't an exact science. She left a bed, a television, a couch, and a cassette player, which I turn on. Paul Simon is singing "Graceland," something about losing love and everybody knows you're hurting. I'm hurting, but nobody knows except my mom, and of course, my wife. At this moment, I understand Simon's message clearly.

Getting through the week between Christmas and New Year's is tough. My fishing buddy, Alex, and his wife, Jennifer, take me for a drink at a restaurant. These are nice people who care about me. We've ordered. Jennifer, sensing I'm doing OK, asks, "How are you getting along, Tom?" Until that moment, I thought I was doing fine. Without warning, I pull a Patsy Cline--I fall to pieces.

The first major loneliness test is New Year's Eve. My wife and I never made this night a big deal, but when you're alone it becomes one. My sister and her husband bail me out--we eat, drink, and listen to oldies at their house. When the Times Square ball drops on California television, I'm asleep. Solo.

Friends tell me, "You need time to heal, to be alone, to reflect." I've never done well sitting around feeling sorry for myself. My wife hadn't died, that would have been different. I plan to pick up the pieces immediately, even if it just means going through some motions of getting out of the house.

"My healing starts right now," I tell my friends, "leading the recovery will be dating." I know I'm probably kidding myself, but my ass is out there.

## Reader Comments and Tom's Responses

Jose: "I thought I'd be looking ahead to sharing older years with my mate. Now, like you, I'm alone. Response: *We'll just tackle this problem together.*

Nancy: "You'll find if you go places without a mate, you'll be treated differently." Response: *Treated better or worse?*

Harriett: "Thank God for animals and television--they are my substitute companions." Response: *You mean that's all I have to look forward to? Does anybody have my wife's phone number? Perhaps I can convince her to come back.*

## Column 2

# MIDDLE AGE DATING OPTIONS AND PROBABILITIES

It's early January. My wife and I separated Christmas Eve. That's not a totally correct statement. She decided to leave on that day. I didn't know we were separated until the morning after Christmas. That's when she told me. Time is slipping away--I've decided to start dating immediately.

Each day my hair is more silver; my face more wrinkled. I can't break eight minutes in the mile anymore. My heart is empty. I want some female companionship.

But where does a new middle aged single begin? I'm fortunate, I guess. I own a deli in a California beach town. Many attractive women pass through the deli doors each day. In the summer, bikinis are plentiful. But this isn't summer, it's winter.

I jot down 10 appealing female customers I would enjoy taking out. I think this middle-aged dating life may be like shooting fish in a barrel. Who knows? I might even be up to dating speed in two or three weeks. Perhaps the big hurt will be avoided altogether.

As any organized person about to tackle a new pursuit, I get focused. To keep the potential dates' names straight, a list is started entitled: **Deli Women To Date**.

Effortlessly, the 10 names are affixed, ranked in descending order of desirability. I rub my hands together as if I'm about to sit down to a feast. It never crosses my mind that dating deli customers could have disastrous consequences. When one's desperate, one doesn't think about that kind of stuff.

As the 10 women, and many others come in, I casually and sometimes not so casually mention I'm now single and eligible. To my chagrin, none seem to take the bait.

I hear all kinds of excuses why they decline to go out. The most frequently stated is: "I'm seeing someone." Reality starts to tell me this return to dating at age 54 isn't going to be quite as easy as I first thought.

Why aren't 28 to 35 year-old women flipping over me? Maybe I'm not the stud I thought I was 10 to 20 years before.

My problem: I've got a 54 year-old's face, a 45 year-old's body (I hope) with a 25 year-old's mentality towards women.

After going 0 for 10 on the **Deli Women To Date** list, I rename it the **Prospects** list. I rearrange the ranking order from desirability to probability of getting a date. My new rule: Any woman's name in this county can be added. At least, I'm being more realistic by expanding the search beyond the deli.

The first thing a new single gets is advice. Plenty of it. From my 82 year-old mom: "Don't date any more women with kids. You've been down that route before."

"But Mom," I argue, "everyone in the middle age dating arena carries some baggage around. If I exclude women with kids, the potential dating pool shrinks by about 90 percent."

Mom admits that women with grown kids are OK, "...as long as the kids are out of the roost."

Mom has another piece of advice, "Beware of committing adultery. Don't bring any women home. Your wife may be having you watched."

"What?" I protest. When I was thinking of how green the grass would be dating again, not bringing women home wasn't on the other side of the fence.

Then Terry, my friend of 30 years, takes me aside: "Tom, are you aware of the dangers of AIDS and other sexually transmitted diseases? Have you confronted this danger? My opinion: You shouldn't date at all."

Terry's a bright guy. He's been the VP-Marketing of the San Diego Visitors and Convention Bureau for over 12 years. He sounds like a saint. Years ago when he and I worked together for American Airlines, he wasn't. I've always respected his opinion, but he has lost it on this one.

Now I'm depressed. Let's see, I shouldn't date women with kids still living at home, and the two big "A's"--adultery and AIDS-- are obviously to be avoided.

Hell, maybe Terry's right--I shouldn't even date. Maybe I should reconcile with my wife. I can see this new life just ain't going to be no fun at all.

My lawyer explains that adultery doesn't exist in California--the only grounds for dissolution of marriage are irreconcilable differences or in curable insanity. "You better have some fun along the way," the lawyer suggests, "because in the end, it's going to cost you lots of money, and you might just end up insane."

My lawyer's words got rid of one of the big "A's." That advice was worth the $300 per hour I paid him. Next, I need to address the other big "A." AIDS. I'll do that next week.

## Reader Comments and Tom's Responses

Judith: "Was it a joke or did I miss the point--you wanting to date 28 to 35 year-olds, women 19 to 26 years younger? Under 45 is too young for you. Grow up and get real." Response: *When I started to date, I didn't think first about how old a prospect was. Any woman who wasn't nailed to the floor, from age 20 to 80, I'd ask out. As time goes on, you'll see a change.*

Ken: "You're a wimp, get out there and date." Response: *Hey, Ken, cut me some slack, my wife of 7 years left only a couple of weeks ago.*

Gay: "Keep your eyes open for dating opportunities all of the time." Response: *That's sage advice.*

Joan: "You should wait one to two years before dating. Sit back, look at who you are, learn to like yourself, then date." Response: *I already like myself. Mother, may I go out?*

## Column 3

# CONDOM SHOPPING: AN EMBARRASSING TRIP

In my last column, I mentioned the two big "A's." Adultery was addressed. Now AIDS will be. I never dreamed at age 54 I'd have to worry about AIDS or other sexually transmitted diseases.

In my '60s and '70s reckless dating days, penicillin and Perinate 200 cured just about anything. Now, nearly everyday, we hear of someone dying of AIDS.

Friends and relatives warn us that, if we're going to be sleeping with anyone, we're taking a huge risk of contacting AIDS or a serious venereal disease.

Enough said. Now, singles need to be extra cautious before hopping in the sack. Darn, it used to be so much fun.

One of the first orders of business before becoming sexually involved with anybody is to protect ourselves. This is as equally important for women as for men.

Condoms are a must. Yuck! Disgusting! During my three marriages covering over 14 years, I chuckled smugly when I saw a condom display. "Not for me," I'd think as I snubbed my nose, "those condoms are only for promiscuous singles." Egad, now I'm single. I've always been and still am a pretty horny guy. If a person is going to date, AIDS should quickly become a major concern in the jungle of dating.

11

# MIDDLE AGED AND DATING AGAIN

Condom shopping is necessary, but I've looked forward to root canals more. Reluctantly, I'm off to Longs Drugs--pharmacy section.

As a kid, buying those slippery devils made me nervous. We only purchased them so we wouldn't "knock up" some woman. I never understood why we called an unmarried woman getting pregnant as being "knocked up." I remember going to the drug store and saying, "My parents want me to pick up some rubbers for them."

That's what we called condoms back then--rubbers. I'd choke on the dirty word. Did the pharmacist believe me? Of course not. He probably didn't even sell them to me. I'd pay someone else to buy them. It was sort of the same deal as when we'd have a guy over age 21 buy booze for us.

Even then, I could never figure them out, get them on right, nor did I really comprehend their purpose. Who am I kidding? I never got laid until I was 21 and then I paid for it--a call girl in the Soho District in London. I recall she stealthily whipped on a condom with one hand while holding *The London Times* she was reading with the other. More clearly I recall the four inch knife scare across her face. A home-town buddy shared her with me for four English pounds. When we see each other now, 37 years later, we still snap our fingers, indicating the short amount of time each of us lasted with her.

Buying condoms today is no more comfortable for me than trying to buy them as a teen-ager. I enter the store. Twice I walk pass condom central. I know it's there, I've been in this store over 50 times. It's amazing that condoms are in a section all by themselves now. In the old days, druggists hid them in a drawer behind the counter.

I am here purposely in the early morning to avoid a crowded store. When no one else is in the aisle, I move in. The choices are mind boggling. I thought there were only a couple of different kinds. Now there are large, medium, extra thin, ribbed, spermicidally lubricated, latex, natural, blue, brown, mint flavored, glow-in-the-dark, dry, snug, extra snug--what's going on here? How do I choose? More importantly, how do I choose quickly before my next door neighbor walks by? If that happened, I'd probably say, "I'm buying them for my teen-age kids," but, I'd be lying--I don't have children.

This isn't like shopping for a pair of shoes. One doesn't ask the pharmacist, "What do you have in a size 10, extra wide, thin at the ankle?" Nor do you sit down, try some on, walk around to judge how they feel, and ask your mom how they look.

I pick two boxes, a dozen dry, a dozen wet. Sounds like I'm going fly fishing. I'd rather be. Guess in a way I am. Fly fishing's easier. I'd rather tie on a minuscule size-22 fly to my leader than roll on a condom. Anyway, I have two dozen nasty critters in my bare hands. Optimistic aren't I? I can't imagine working for a condom manufacturer.

Relieved, I move to the hair coloring section for a tube of Grecian Formula 44. Now it's called Grecian Formula 16. What happened to 44? Why did the manufacturer deduct 28 numbers from the name? Toothpaste, a toothbrush, and a few other unneeded items are grabbed. I have no plans to darken my silver hair, but someday I'll be able to use the toothpaste and toothbrush. I'm buying the other stuff for smoke screens, to make the condoms less conspicuous at check-out.

Now the awkward part. I approach the cashier. A woman gets in line behind me. I pretend I forgot something so she will go ahead of me. I return. Just as I feared, the cashier's a woman.

Placing the items on the counter, I find myself whistling. I haven't whistled since summoning a taxi in New York City in 1971.

I try to divert the cashier's attention, "Nice day isn't it?" She smiles while routinely passing each item over a scanner. Thank God for scanners, she probably isn't aware of what I'm purchasing.

Horror--the box of lubricated condoms doesn't scan. The cashier looks at it and swipes it a couple more times. Suddenly, it's like being in a dream. I know what she's going to do next, but I can't stop her. She reaches for the store microphone alongside the register. She pushes the control button to the **on** position. I try to speak but words don't come out. Her voice reverberates throughout the store, **"Price check. Trojans--ENZ, latex condoms."** I about die. Why did she have to do that? Now she knows exactly what I'm getting, as does everybody else in the store.

But the worse isn't over. The pharmacist replies, **"What size?"** Then, she speaks again, **"Just medium."** I'm blown away, what does she mean, "Just medium?" How can she tell by looking at me that I'm only, "Just medium?"

The pharmacist responds, **"The box. What size is the box?"** I feel like I'm trapped near the net of a game of prophylactic ping pong, only the ball is made out of latex. Back and forth, back and forth. I decide I don't want to be single anymore. If my wife walked in, I'd take her back. No I wouldn't. I swear women's heads are popping up from behind all the aisles. She replies, "**12-pack, lubricated. It's the light blue box.**" The pharmacist finally ends the agony, "**$6.73.**"

The cashier turns off the microphone. She says nothing to me. I know she's thinking: "Dating again sir?" I am mentally drained. I feel like the space shuttle crew on the launch pad when the mission is aborted at the last second.

Leaving the pharmacy, I look to ensure no one I know saw me. At least I'm armed and ready for action, with no place to go. And I still can't get them on right. I seem to roll them on inside-out. Ouch! They ought to put a label in them, like they do for a plastic bag: "Open here."

A few of them are hidden in the glove box of the car, the rest in the night stand next to my bed. Ridiculous for a 54 year-old man to be doing this. A few months go by, the condoms haven't been disturbed. I wonder if over time they crumple and turn to dust?

Once, a date tried to locate a road map in the glove box of my car. Fearing she would find the condoms, I almost broke her hand trying to slam the door shut.

People who are dating need to protect themselves. The thought of using condoms may be distasteful, but they are a fact of life if one is to sleep with others.

## Reader Comments and Tom's Responses

Rebecca: "Disgusting. You and your wife separated three weeks ago and already you're out buying condoms. What's wrong with you? **Response:** *I'm only following the advice of my lawyer.*

Sherrie: "Do men really think of these things so early after separation?" **Response:** *Yes. Most of us would rather be armed and safe than unarmed and dangerous.*

William: "Been there, done that." **Response:** *The things we do for love.*

## Column 4

# THE SAD REALITY OF DATING HITS EARLY

After Separation Day, three miserable, lonely, stay-at-home, sit-in-bars, weeks go by. No dates. No prospects. No nothing. **That grass that I thought would be greener is grayer.**

Re-emerging into the dating world is difficult. You don't just pick up where you left off before entering your last relationship. Thinking back, I wasn't in such great shakes then either. And now I'm 7 years older.

The traditional singles' bar scene is out. I decide the lounge at the world-famous Ritz Carlton Hotel isn't a traditional bar so I go there. It's only a half-mile from my house. If I have too many adult beverages, I can walk home. Perhaps I'll meet some wealthy woman who's lonely--I think I'm desperate.

Now being single, I have to budget my money. I park in the Salt Creek Beach parking lot 100 yards from the hotel. There, a quarter buys 20 minutes in the parking meters, cheaper by far than the hotel's valet service. Besides, my Suzuki Sidekick seems out of character being parked by guys wearing white gloves.

My Ritz M.O.: I walk through the large lounge area. If there are no women, I leave. If there are women, without men, I sit near them in a couch or chair. I pretend to read *The Wall Street Journal.*

17

Alcoholic beverages are expensive here, so a glass of soda water is ordered--$2. Approaching women at the Ritz is awkward. One needs to be creative.

I've never had any luck at the Ritz so I don't go there anymore. The bar's pretty dead. A bar is still a bar, even if it's located in one of the most beautiful settings in the world. The next time I go to the Ritz will be with a date, if I can get one.

### Mistaken identity

A regular customer at the deli tells me a woman in his office named Debbie is available. He tells me Debbie comes to the deli often.

I know Debbie--I'd love to take her out. He says he'll say something to her. I add her name to the "Prospects" list.

A few days pass. No Debbie. A week later he returns, "Debbie came here but you didn't say anything to her. Now she's embarrassed." I'm befuddled. Debbie didn't come in.

We uncover the mystery: mistaken identity on my part. I thought he was talking about a different Debbie. The embarrassed Debbie comes in a week later. She's attractive. I suggest, "Let's go out." She refuses.

The other Debbie comes in the next day. I ask her out. She's getting married the next month to a deli customer. I remove her from the "Prospects" list.

## Trying again

A second dating opportunity presents itself in the deli. A woman customer I haven't seen since Separation Day comes in. Mary is about 50, classy, attractive, and is not wearing a wedding ring. She's always pleasant and orders carrot juice.

Mary is not on the "Prospects" list because frankly I'd forgotten about her. I need to think fast because she's leaving soon. A story is fabricated.

I say, "The last time you were here a handsome gentleman asked if you were married. I told him I didn't know." She seemed surprised. "Tom, you know I've been married to Richard for 28 years, don't you?"

Richard eats at my deli 5 times a week--tuna salad sandwich and a coke. He's a great guy. I never put the two together.

I respond, "I never knew that. The gentleman will be disappointed." I don't think she suspects I was asking for myself. Sometimes, I'm such a dunce.

## Reader Comments and Tom's Responses

Jo: "There are a few good things about being 55--cheaper movies, and some restaurant discounts. But being single, over 55, and a woman, is an almost impossible situation." Response: *It's about as bad for men of that age.*

Maxine: "Divorce is not fatal. Get off the pity potty." Response: *Give me a little bit of a break, I've only been separated a month.*

Lillian: "There are lots of nice women out there to date and I'm one of them." Response: *Yes, but how do we find each other?*

Eddie: "Every woman I've dated is either a woman's libber or a nut case. I'd rather sit home and watch paint dry. Good luck. And if you're really lucky, you won't be going out period." Response: *Eddie, You're taking this dating thing much too seriously.*

Anonymous woman: "You can't get any kind of a date because you're some kind of a pervert, hanging around and probably harassing younger women. I'm turning 50. I'm very beautiful. I would never, ever, ever, ever, go out with someone as screwed up as you." Response: *How can I call you for a date when you didn't leave your phone number?*

## Column 5

# MAYBE NEXT TIME HE WILL MARRY A DOG

It's the end of January--a month since Separation Day. Loneliness has got me. This middle-aged guy has tried to get out there without much luck.

People, especially women, keep telling me to date ladies near my own age. I suppose they're right.

Maybe I'll paste a note on my forehead or carry a sign that reads: **WANTED TO DATE: 45-55 YEAR-OLD WOMAN.**

A more pressing problem is getting a date with a woman of *any age*.

A couple of years ago, when I was working in real estate, I hated to come home to a beeping answering machine. It usually meant someone wanted a real estate favor for free. Now when I come home, I pray for a beep, hoping some woman wants to go out. Or just talk. Or breathe. Or sigh.

But there are never any messages. Just hang-ups. Probably telemarketers--they always hang up. Maybe I could get a date with one of them?

Perhaps I should run one of those love-connection ads. Don't think so. Not yet at least.

My wife was a teetotaler so I seldom drank. We never even had booze around the house. If I had a nip, she'd complain, and say I smelled of alcohol and make me sleep on the couch.

The other day, she stopped over for one of those downer settlement discussions separated couples have. She opened the refrigerator to get some milk for her coffee.

There were six bottles of chardonnay on the bottom shelf, and three white zinfandels and two bottles of champagne on the shelf above that. Various selections of beer were crammed in here and there. She didn't see the vodka in the freezer. She said nothing. A few days later, based on what she saw in the refrigerator, she told her hairdresser that I now have a drinking problem.

Sure, I have a couple of glasses of wine on occasion. But those bottles of wine aren't for me. They lie waiting for the hoped-for time when I'll entertain women at home. My wife doesn't understand my intention, which is just fine. I'd prefer she believe I have a drinking problem.

Separations change one's priorities. The landscape around the house deteriorates. The lawn doesn't get cut. I don't care. Neighbors on both sides have mowed the grass. Not that they feel sorry for me, they just know I'm not going to do it.

My surfing priority has changed also. Before Separation Day, I surfed at least once a week. I haven't surfed in a month. There are now different demands on my time.

I've lost six pounds. Pretty much I'm a wreck, but I keep telling people, "I'm fine." When a new single says, "I'm fine," you can bet they are hurting--it's the biggest fib a new single tells. Besides, friends don't want to hear how miserable a person is.

I have to keep picking myself up. On some days it's easier than others. Sometimes a good cry just happens. The thought of starting over again at age 54 is pretty devastating, no matter how tough I think I am. I remind myself I'm lucky--I'm healthy and I have my friends.

The mindsets of marriage are hard to change. When my wife lived here, she never allowed the dogs in the house. Now, I remind myself that it's OK. It's my house, I can do what I want. I can even have a cocktail here if I want one.

I hug my two dogs a lot. They sense something isn't right because momma isn't around. They feel my sadness so they seem to care more about me than before.

Maybe next time I'll marry a dog.

## Reader Comments and Tom's Responses

Rosanne: "It's not as hard as your column makes it sound." Response: *You're right, it's harder.*

Bruce: "You'll feel this way for two years." Response: *You mean this fun will last that long?*

John: "Healing doesn't start with the advent of dating. Only time and a new growing, loving relationship will put the hurt on the shelf. You can't rush that." Response: *Do you mean I'm not healing yet?*

## Column 6

# FIRST DATE SHOCKER--SHE'S 26 YEARS YOUNGER

My search for a date finally pays a dividend. Number three on the "Prospects" list agrees to go out. Near my deli cash register, she slips me her business card, saying, "That will be fun."

It's only a little over a month since Separation Day and I have a date with a woman who looks like *Sports Illustrated* cover model Elle McPherson. She's almost as tall. I'll call her Elle.

We go to a restaurant in the harbor for happy hour. When we walk in, every man's eyes focus on this blonde beauty with long hair and long legs. She mentions she made a sales call just prior to our date which probably explains why she's so dressed to kill in a white sweater/skirt outfit.

I have my deli clothes on--a T-shirt, tan shorts, and Reeboks. I smell like an onion. I notice a hint of mustard on my shirt. I wish I had changed for my first date in 8 years.

Immediately, I like Elle. My only concern about Elle becoming my girlfriend is her height. In heels, she's my height. Could that jeopardize our relationship? I wonder if she's even aware of the height similarity? I keep wanting to jump to make myself taller. What's wrong with me? We've been out 15 minutes. Already, I'm fantasizing that she's my woman.

I've had a tough month. If being with Elle is the end result, the pain's been worth it. Who says middle-aged separation has to be such a terrible thing? Hey, endure some pain and then grab the gusto. We only go around once. Have fun.

Ninety minutes later, while walking to the parking lot, Elle says, "Next time, we should go out somewhere in my neighborhood." I can't believe my ears. Elle wants a rematch, near where she lives, I wonder what she has in mind? Her height doesn't seem to matter.

"How about Saturday night?" I waste no time responding. She can't; she has plans to help her mother. Then I make my first error in my new dating career. Like a goof, I say, "I know there is an age difference between us. If that bothers you, I'll understand."

Until that moment, I hadn't considered her age, just her height. Perhaps, at that point, she hadn't considered my age either. Why am I so stupid? As a former salesman, I know better. The sales presentation is going along great. You've got the order. You never, never, introduce a negative, which I just did.

Elle responds, "How old are you?"

Her question catches me off guard. But a salesman is always prepared for objections. I answer, "That's not fair. How old are you?" Not fair? I must be joking. I started this subject of age. Now I sound like a whiner.

"Older than you think," Elle answers. Her response fires me up. Every added year of her age will close our age difference gap. Maybe she's thinking the same. "How old is that?"

"28."

I about collapse in the parking lot.

A quick calculation yields a difference of 26 years. What a shock. My heart falls, but I hide my disappointment. Even if I avoid revealing my age, I know someday, if I meet her parents, the age difference will matter to them. I'm probably older than Elle's mother. I wonder what she looks like? Shame on me for my thoughts. I escape the evening without revealing my age.

At home, I create a new dating list. This one is called the "Currently Dating" list. Ground rules: A woman's name may only be added if we've actually been out. A scheduled first date does not qualify.

Elle's name proudly goes on line one. That night I have trouble sleeping. For the first time in eight years, a woman other than my wife has started my heart.

## Reader Comments and Tom's Responses

Alice: "Who is this sniveling puke? Lighten up a little. Do you want to go out?" Response: *I'm sorry Alice, I'm busy Saturday night. Frankly, you scare me.*

Maria: "Why is it that middle aged geezers want to date 20-year olds? There are many very attractive, sexually active, women in their 50s and beyond." Response: *I'm finding dating women closer to my age is the only way to go.*

## Column 7

# DATING A WOMAN WHO LOOKS LIKE ELLE MCPHERSON

Life is good. I've been separated just over a month and already I'm dating a beautiful woman who reminds me of Elle McPherson. We've been out once. She's considerably younger.

In my teen-age dating days, I knew how to play it cool. Taking a page from back then, I'm waiting to ask her out again. Undoubtedly, she'll wonder why I haven't asked yet.

A few days after our first date, Elle's boss comes into the deli for a sandwich. He says, "Tom, I understand you and Elle had a great time together. When are you going out again? She didn't seem to know."

Amazing. My tactics are working. The second he leaves, I telephone Elle. "Let's go out Thursday night."

She answers, "How delightful. Let me know where to meet you." I had no idea dating again at my age would be this easy. Southern California is so enlightened--people of diverse backgrounds, ages, and races, all blending together in one big dating melting pot.

I want Elle to see my home, thinking, well, it might impress her. There are no plans nor expectations for a romantic evening. But if she offered, I'd probably accept.

# MIDDLE AGED AND DATING AGAIN

On Thursday I call, "I'm cooking you dinner." "How thoughtful," she replies. I leave work at 4:30 p.m. My friend, Mike, who works in the meat department at Hughes Market, cuts two filets especially for me. Even, Mark, the store manager, checks to be sure the steaks are perfect. Both Hughes guys know how important tonight is for me.

They know about my separation. So do a few others at Hughes. It's part of my strategy to meet eligible women. Sort of like networking when looking for a job. Spread the word. Somewhere, somehow, someone's got a nice friend for me to take out.

Hughes Market has a plethora of friendly and attractive women working the cash registers. I've added a couple of them to my "Prospects" list, not by specific name, but only as Hughes #1 and Hughes #2, because I can't figure out which ones don't have boyfriends. All of the women cashiers at Hughes look pretty good to me.

A half pound of fresh shrimp and a couple of fine cheeses are selected for appetizers. Even a box of Stoned Wheat Thins are included. I've never spent so much on hors d'oeuvres. Dating is expensive.

At home, I prepare for my first bachelor-style evening in 8 years. I vacuum, and even dust, before placing the barren kitchen table in front of the living room fireplace.

A half-burned purple candle becomes the table centerpiece. Old wax is peeled away. I can't locate a tablecloth so placemats with unmatched silverware will have to do. However, I find a couple of identical black plates, but one is chipped.

28

The fireplace, which has been inactive, is readied for its first ignition of the year. My cassette player is moved to the living room. New Kenny G. and Jackson Browne tapes are placed nearby.

A Kenwood chardonnay is in the cooler, a Mondavi cabernet awaits the corkscrew. Myer's rum with freshly squeezed orange juice is available upon request. Stolichnaya vodka is in the freezer. I pick a fresh lemon from the tiny tree near the dogs' house.

A six-pack of Coors Light was purchased because that's the brand Elle was drinking the first night we went out. Hopefully, she'll be impressed that I noticed. Things are going so well for me, I'm almost ashamed. Elle will arrive in 30 minutes.

The phone rings. "Tom, this is Elle." My reaction is humorous-- she probably lost the directions. Maybe she wants to come early. Women enjoy being pampered. I feel important.

**"I've developed a sore throat and am going to have to take a rain check."** Shot and hit, that's how I feel.

Instinct tells me to argue, to try to convince her to come anyway so she can see all the work I've done to prepare her dinner. I remain cool, "That's OK. Let's do it another time."

There will be no romantic dinner in Monarch Beach tonight. At least not at my house. My superficial feelings of importance are shattered.

## Reader Comments and Tom's Responses

Phyllis: "I wish that chardonnay in the refrigerator were for me." Response: *I never had anybody over so I sold the wine at a garage sale.*

Anonymous Woman: "Southern California may be enlightened, but, my dear, you're not. Who cares about your home? You're the final package." Response: *You're right. The only party who seems to care about my home is the mortgage company.*

Connie: "You failed with Elle because your motive wasn't pure. You need to give up your liquor and to do volunteer work. The Salvation Army might be good for you since you enjoy cooking so much. You could cook for them." Response: *My motive with Elle was to feed the poor woman. She's pretty skinny, you know. I already cook 7 days a week so I'd prefer not to do more of that. Maybe I could be a bell ringer for the Salvation Army.*

Anonymous woman: "Not only are you disgusting, perverted, nasty, and old, you're also stupid." Response: *I think you've covered all the bases. Rest assured, I'll never cook for you. I imagine no one will.*

And yet another anonymous woman: "You need to climb into the refrigerator with all of that wine. Cool down, pal."
*I think I've struck a chord here.*

## Column 8

# GOOD BYE ELLE. HELLO AMANDA

Slowly I'm recovering from being stood-up by Elle. She avoids me like the plague. I've dusted myself off and am ready to try again.

A soft drink sales rep who comes in the deli once a week shows up. Maybe, just maybe, she's in her late 30s. She's too young for me, but not 26 years younger which Elle was. Perhaps, she's 16 to 18 years younger, too much of an age difference, but dating's been slow lately. I'll call her Amanda.

She's exotic. Her eyes have lots to say, but they aren't talking. She wears glasses. Sometimes glasses accentuate and magnify a woman's eyes, which is the case with Amanda. They make her even prettier.

A full head of sandy blonde hair is swept back, eventually reaching her backside belt loops. A blue uniform shirt hides what appears to be a nice figure. Everything about her is private.

Her personality is subdued--she's all business. Of course, when she comes in the deli, she's on business. She's professional and thorough, the best sales rep who calls on me. She heads right for that soft drink cooler to check the inventory. She doesn't smile or say much.

I usually just growl at sales reps. With Amanda, I take the time to come around the counter to speak with her. Away from a business environment, I think she'd be fun to date.

31

After pestering her a few times, Amanda agrees to a date. She lives in Laguna Beach. I decide to take her to The Royal Hawaiian, a casual restaurant on Pacific Coast Highway, near where she lives.

Maybe we'll share a la pu la pu, the restaurant's special rock 'em-sock 'em, 6-different rums, drink. That might relax her. Maybe she'll lighten up. My goal for the evening: To get her to go out again. I feel that silly teen-age excitement of a first date.

At home, I dig out an old Waylon Jennings album, "The Ramblin' Man." The last song on side one is *Amanda*. Waylon sings that fate should have made her a gentleman's wife. It's a beautiful, haunting song with lots of steel guitar. I wonder if she's ever heard it. I place the tape in my car stereo, positioned for the song to begin when the radio gets turned on. Then, I wonder if she even knows who Waylon Jennings is?

Amanda's from Palm Springs. I can't get a handle on women from Palm Springs. Why, being so young, would she have lived out there? Did a sugar daddy take care of her? There's something mysterious about her.

The afternoon of our scheduled date, the phone is quiet in the deli. I hope it won't ring, not even for phone-in orders. I don't want Amanda to cancel.

By 2:00 p.m., no call from Amanda--good; 3:00 p.m., no call from Amanda--better yet. *Quit worrying* I tell myself, *I'm the client, she won't cancel.*

At 4:10 p.m., the phone rings. It's Amanda. "I'm stuck at a customer's in Riverside. I have no idea when I'll get home. I'll have to cancel."

I counter, "Why don't I pick you up an hour later?" I refuse to throw in the towel as easily as I did with Elle. This broken date business just isn't going to happen to me anymore.

"By then, it'll be too late. I have to go to Palm Springs tomorrow...The traffic on the 91 Freeway is bad.." Excuses keep flowing from her pretty mouth.

"Call me when you get home," I tell her, refusing to let her off the hook. We hang up.

I wanted a chance, that's all. No raincheck was offered. She doesn't want to go out. Ever.

I wonder why she made a date in the first place? I'm disappointed. How silly, I'm a big boy now. This is all a part of the roller coaster called dating again at middle age. Get up. Get crushed. Get up. Get flattened. I feel like a piece of asphalt.

This was my fault. Amanda's too young for me. No, I'm too old for her. I can't blame her. I rationalize--maybe she just didn't want to mix business with pleasure.

Someday, I'll ask her. Fate won't make her this gentleman's wife.

# MIDDLE AGED AND DATING AGAIN

## Reader Comments and Tom's Responses

Tricia: "I was at a singles club. Everybody was about 25. Where do middle aged and dating people gather?" Response: *This seems to be the most frequently asked question. We need to find a centrally located banquet type room where we can gather perhaps one night per month. Let's make it our mission. To get in, people would have to show i.d. No one under 40 allowed. To keep the ratio balanced, bring a friend of the opposite sex you aren't dating (unless, of course, you'd like to dump the one you are dating).*

Tamara: "I cringed when I read in your last column, 'Did a sugar daddy take care of her?' You'll never have any success dating with that kind of attitude." Response: *What was wrong with the question? I was just speculating why she lived in Palm Springs. It had nothing to do with Amanda, she's a sweetheart.*

Steve: "Is this column for real or are you a comedian? You need help from a professional bachelor--which I used to be. First, never date your customers or business associates. You need their money and they won't come back. Second, make all of your dates for lunch or afternoon tea. That way, if they break them, you haven't wasted an entire evening. Also, lunches are cheaper than dinners and the women won't drink as much. Third, meet your women through friends. Just ask if they have a friend, that's the best way to meet people your age. Don't go for bimbos, there's no future in it. I'm married now, so I can't give you too much first-hand advice." Response: *Wow. I wish I'd have written all of that. Good advice.*

## Column 9

# THE FIRST MONTHS OF DATING AGAIN AT AGE 54

I've been dating now for six months. I realize there's still lots more to learn, but here are a few of the lessons learned so far:

**Lesson one:** Whether you're a man or a woman, when you're middle aged and dating again, be prepared for rejection. Lots of it. There were four Friday nights in a row when women broke dates. Why do they do that?

**Lesson Two:** If one's expectations are unrealistic, there will be even more rejection. For me, trying to date younger women is the number one unrealistic expectation.

A little younger is OK. A lot younger is foolish. Last week I dined with a couple--he's 47, she's 23. She proclaimed at the table, "I don't even know how old he is, nor do I care." As the night wore on and the wine went down, the reasons she didn't care emerged. Let's see, could his ocean front Laguna Beach pad, the trip to Australia he's taking her on, his 50-case wine cellar, frequent dinners out, or his BMW 750i, have anything to do with it? She gets the material things; he gets the young body.

Everything's fine until the money runs out. When that happens, so will she.

How can there be compatibility when you're buying a golf cart for a commute vehicle and she wants a Ferrari?

Elle was 26 years younger than I. For me, it wasn't a macho or insecurity thing. She just looked great and had a pleasant manner. And she was the first woman to agree to go out with me, even if it was for just a total of 90 minutes. The bad news. I never got to check out her mother. That's who I should have dated.

For a middle-ager, I was not being realistic. The "Prospects" list contained names of just long shots--women I wanted to take out because I was physically attracted to them--who had no interest in me.

The list was wishful thinking--it was peppered with the names of women who were too young. Those women didn't want to go out with a guy who will reach senior citizen status later this year. I can't blame them.

When you're a 30-year old woman, do you want to be kissed by a 54 year-old guy whose breath smells like kerosene? Disgusting.

As for me, I want someone who can remember where they were standing when they heard that JFK had been shot, and when Armstrong walked on the moon. Someone who knows 20 Mule Team Borax was a cleanser and not a rock group.

"Stand in the mirror," I told myself, "look at the age in your eyes; the color of your hair. Throw on a little Grecian Formula you bought at the pharmacy and go find some women nearer to your age."

The lecture to myself continued: "Expand your horizons beyond the deli and the Hughes Market. Try the bank, the Shell gas station, Home Base, Price Club, the harbor, the mall, and even church." Church? Did I say church? Let's not get carried away here, Tom.

Men who try to date younger women stir up quite a reaction from females. One woman in Laguna Beach accused me of being a child molester. Another woman called me a *sniveling puke*.

**Lesson three:** Just because time passes, it doesn't mean you're not lonely anymore.

It has been six months since Separation Day, and it's just plain lonely. Readers give advice: "Take time to heal, to like yourself. Don't date for two years." Hogwash. I'd rather be out and miserable than home and miserable. Some of us are meant to have a partner. If I can't share with Susan, I'll share with Romona.

If I hear, "It takes six months to heal for every two years you were together..." one more time, I'll leave immediately for Mustang Ranch.

**Lesson four:** Just because we've learned these lessons doesn't mean we always follow them. I found out through my experience with Elle that going out with younger women isn't a good idea. So what did I do? I asked out Amanda.

A friend tells me at least I haven't started wearing gold chains and calling everybody "babe." There's hope.

## Reader Comments and Tom's Responses

Lisa: "Why didn't you get back with your wife? You're doing a great job. Your column is entertaining and it's refreshing to hear the man's perspective. Response: *Similar to what Elton John sang about Norma Jean, our candle burned out long before our marriage ever did. My wife left with no notice, I didn't want to get back together after she did that.*

Denise: "For men, dating someone younger can work. When I was 25, I married a man who was 27 years older. We had a wonderful 10 years before he passed away." Response: *Age is just a state of mind. But, Denise, and I'm not being disrespectful, what ultimately happened in your situation illustrates one of the negatives of dating someone considerably older—you may lose them.*

Mrs. B: "Hang in there and look for a very dear friend. Someone you want to spend a life with and not just a night with." Response: *Having been married three times, that's the wisest advice I've ever heard. Getting married after a one night stand just isn't smart.*

Jeffrey (woman): "When I divorced, I had two young daughters so I didn't date. Now they are older, I need to start my life. Being single is all new to me, it's a struggle. Usually, I pay my own way, but sometimes I pay for both of us." Response: *Many women give up dating to concentrate on raising their kids. I respect that highly. You are the type of woman I want to meet. You are grounded in what is right.*

## Column 10

# GET YOURSELF A BUDDY--BUT NO HANKY-PANKY

The night Amanda cancels the date, I'm depressed. I just can't sit home alone. I call Shirley. She's a buddy. When one becomes single again, regardless of age or sex, it's helpful to have a buddy,

Buddies are particularly useful in the early stages of being alone when nobody else seems to care.

I define a **buddy** as someone of the opposite sex with whom one can freely talk, drink, dine, or take walks. The key ingredient: no physical hanky-panky.

Buddy rules are understood often without even being discussed. They are mutually agreed upon but often it's the woman who dictates them. The guy has a choice to accept the nothing-physical aspect or go find another buddy.

Buddies usually don't fall in love--they're too much like advisers. They're open, honest, even critical. They can say what they want without worrying that what they say will hurt the other person's feelings. Neither tries to impress the other.

I ask Shirley, "What should I do about Amanda? I've been trying to get a date with her for months and then she cancels on me. I told her to call me when she gets home."

"Leave her a message that you understand she's tied up so you've gone ahead and made other plans. Be nice about it. She'll understand you're not a whimp."

Shirley's right. No matter how much I want to go out with Amanda, I must take a stand.

Shirley says she'll come over for a glass of wine. Unlike Elle, Shirley's not afraid to come to my house. She's 5'7", pretty, witty, and intelligent. She appears to be of independent means. She's about 20 years younger and wants children, and a man her age or younger.

Shirley's also got the blues. She owns an ocean view townhome overlooking a blue ocean. The home has powder blue carpet. She drives a blue BMW with a car phone. Her license plate reads BMURBLU. A blue point Himalayan cat named "Beamer" usually occupies the blue leather passenger seat.

She's also blue because she's unemployed. Cutbacks in the defense industry ambushed her $100,000+ vp-sales position.
Her search for a new job is taking longer than planned, so sometimes she's discouraged about that.

She's even more blue because she still likes her ex-boyfriend who's younger than she. I used to tell her the guy's a lost cause, but she doesn't want to hear that anymore. None of us likes bad news. We shoot the messenger. Or worse, our buddy.

A buddy is like having a shrink. Only having a buddy is cheaper and more fun. You talk. They listen. Sometimes they talk, you listen. The money goes for cocktails and food instead of in the shrink's pocket.

We've been to dinner a couple of times. We alternate paying. I'm glad we're just buddies--it's better that way.

She's been to my house before. She parks her BMW in front. A couple of neighbors have mentioned seeing her and the car. They think Tom's dating a younger, flashy female. Of course, that's not the case. I know it bugs the neighbor who is my ex-wife's friend.

We drink two bottles of wine and eat a large bag of parmesan cheese-flavored potato chips. Shirley gives me some advice, the best I've received from anyone so far: "With these women you're dating or trying to date, expect nothing. That way, you'll not be disappointed. If something good happens, it will be a pleasant surprise." Shirley's advice is wise for me, I come across as a little too desperate.

Shirley leaves. I pass out on the couch that John and Janine, my favorite neighbors, gave me. I think they felt sorry for me because the house was so empty after my wife left.

An hour later, I wake myself by getting sick on one of the cushions. Too much white wine and too many potato chips. How disgusting. Fraternity behavior. Just because I'm 54, I'm not immune to doing stupid things. I wonder what all my successful fraternity brothers would think if they could see me now.

Having a buddy has been good for me. Hopefully, the feeling is mutual for her. Now that I'm further along in the healing process, I don't see her as often. I try to spend my time with women who might become potential girlfriends.

When a new partner enters one's life, buddies tend to fade into the sunset. New partners don't like old buddies hanging around, they always think something sexual happened.

## Reader Comments and Tom's Responses

Judy: "You seem like a typical self-pitying male, but you're intelligent and write a good column. Stop looking for a woman to make you happy. Make yourself happy first, and then look for a woman. Do you want to go out? Response: *I'm already happy. The right woman might make me happier.*

Charlotte and Joe: "Forget the women, let's play golf." Response: *I need a woman to complete the foursome.*

Clint: "I have a job for your buddy Shirley." Response: *Shirley just got a job, but I'll pass the information on to her.*

Bobbie: "You're having a rough time, old chap. Care to share a cup of tea with me?" Response: *Tea gives me the shakes—I even dilute my Snapple drinks.*

Anonymous woman: Regarding Shirley, you act as if money is a big deal! Who cares where Shirley lives, what she made, and what she drives. If she's a good friend--great. Tom, you're trying too hard. Relax, it will all happen in due time." Response: *I'll bet Shirley cares where she lives, what she made, and what she drives.*

## Column 11

# REFLECTIONS ON DIVORCE #3

I signed the divorce papers recently. The marriage will be formally dissolved in a few months.

I have mixed emotions. For me, it's the third divorce. I told my mom I would never get married again. She said, "Never, say never." So now I'm saying I probably won't do it again. I'm not proud of three divorces. At least, I was decisive enough to make the marriage decision three times.

This marriage started off so well. I met her in Dallas, a real Texas cutie. She was originally from Ohio, but had acquired a Southern accent. You know, always "fixin" to do this and "fixin" to do that. At the start, I thought it was neat. In the end, I thought it was put on and enough to make one puke. We lived in California for seven years together.

I proposed to her by having a biplane fly over my Northern California house dragging a banner, "S-----, will you marry me?" A local radio station got wind of it, and encouraged her on the air to accept. They even interviewed her. The neighbors wrote, "say yes," at the top of the driveway.

We came to Orange County six years ago. I started a business with both of our nicknames on the front sign: "Tutor and Spunky's Deli." We bought a Suzuki Samurai, which was one of those silly little dreams married couples have. It was our fun car. Everything we did as a couple was cute. I helped raise her two boys.

43

On Xmas Eve., two years ago, the three of them decided they'd had enough. They cleaned out the house and took off. They failed to tell me first. Since Separation Day, I've seen one of the boys. That's pretty sad. For awhile, I believed I was positioned by God to take care of them, to see that they got a good home. I don't believe that anymore, because God wouldn't have scripted a finish like the one that happened.

I will never be a number 2 or number 3 in a woman's pecking order again. She always said blood was thicker than water.

Over time, we just drifted apart. There were no fights, cheats or uglies. I just stopped trying and caring. Separation was probably inevitable by springtime of 1994. Maybe she felt running from the problem was easier than facing it, and discussing it. The biggest bitterness I have is how she left.

We each hired lawyers, but we settled out of court. Lawyers' fees were still about $4000--hard earned money down the tube. A friend Doug just paid his lawyer $18,000. His wife's probably racked up about the same amount. They haven't even gone to court yet. A fraternity brother told me his divorce settlement was $450,000. I guess he's been more financially successful than I.

I got stuck with the house. Normally, that would be good. But in Orange County, home values have plunged in the last five years so there's no equity left, but a $290,000 mortgage remains.. Financially, I'm strapped.

When my two previous marriages soured, I adopted breakup songs which were popular at the time. First marriage breakup song: Barbara Streisand, *The Way We Were.* Second marriage breakup song: Streisand again, this time with Neil Diamond, *You Don't Bring Me Flowers Anymore.*

This marriage breakup song: R.E.M., *Everybody Hurts.* So there I was a few weeks back, watching the movie, "When A Man Loves A Woman." During the park scene when he is leaving her to move to Denver, *Everybody Hurts* comes on. My defenses were down. My eyes began to tear. Little ones at first--the kind that make it hard to focus. Bigger tears followed, which rolled down my front, filling my belly button. My date didn't know what to do.

Time flies. The divorce will be final before the O.J. Simpson trial begins.

I have to make a new start, to get on with life. For me, it will be hard to build a trusting relationship with a woman. I'm not the type who enjoys going it alone. Someday, somehow, there will be another special woman in my life. I wonder if I know her? I'll be out there looking.

# Reader Comments and Tom's Responses

Janet: "I've been married four times. I appreciate your courage. You just open your stomach and let your guts fall out for all of the world to see. I think we could be friends. Response: *You've had one more marriage than I. I'd be afraid of someone with that much more experience.*

Loretta: "Lovely column. I saw you in the Hughes Market parking lot. I give you a lot of credit--you give us hope. You're very good looking for your age." Response: *Are you sure you saw me, not someone else? Why did you have to add, "for your age?"*

Patti: "Your best column ever. I still get tears in my eyes when I watch the movie classic, *An Affair To Remember*." Response: *Anyone who hasn't seen that movie should rent it immediately. It's one of the greatest love stories of all times.*

Judy: "I was surprised and impressed to learn that you can cry." Response: *A person who can cry has the capability to be deeply touched. I think that's a pretty important quality in a man or a woman.*

Steve: "I'm 58, a professional single. I've tried it all--computer dating, visual dating, and television dating. Finally, I hired a professional dating service. What you should be doing is going to the things you enjoy most, and that's where you'll meet the woman of your dreams." Response: *You are precisely right, Steve. People need to get out of the house and do things. That's the only way to meet people.*

## Column 12

# ANOTHER YOUNGER WOMAN SAYS NO

A woman whose name is near the top of the "Prospects" list works at the Price Club. She has no idea she's on such a list. Her name is Spritzer.

Spritzer's a beauty--boney nose, high cheek bones, clear complexion, small waist, tight fanny, and a sizeable chest. Had she been around in my college days, she would have been called a **"stone-cold fox."** But, she wasn't born yet. So, here I am, checking out a younger one again.

To provision my deli, I've been going to Price Club weekly for five years. I used to despise going, but now that I'm single, I can't wait to go.

Spritzer's just one of the many attractive and pleasant women working there. Another is Gloria. What a sweetheart. She wears the warmest smile I've ever seen. Gloria's married.

Also, whole bunches of pretty women shop there. It's a great place to hang out. I've gone to Price Club so much lately my deli is overstocked.

I've known Spritzer for five years. We always make silly, small talk. I've tried to explain to her that I'm now single and available, but she's always too busy for me to finish my pitch.

# MIDDLE AGED AND DATING AGAIN

Lately, I've made a few unnecessary trips to Price Club, hoping to catch Spritzer working at a slow time so I can finish the pitch. I park, walk in. If she's working the register, I'll buy a couple of items and stand in her line, even if it's the longest.

I finally got the chance to say, "Let's go out." She said she was booked every night for the next two weeks except for two weeks from Friday. Foolishly, I said that was too far in advance to plan. I still don't know why I said that. After all, good things are worth waiting for. The two weeks came and went in a flash.

Slowly, I'm realizing that Spritzer and Tom aren't going to happen. Then, one day she passes me in the pickles' aisle, "I need to talk to you. Get me in my check-out line up front."

I'm elated. Obviously, she's come to her senses and probably wants to go out. She must finally realize she needs a mature man after working around all of these younger people.

Waiting in her line, I find myself whistling again, just as I did waiting in the line at the pharmacy when I was buying condoms. She winks at me. There is really something up her sleeve. I wonder if I should play a little hard to get.

It seems like an eternity getting to her staging area. Planning ahead, I think I'll take her to Las Brisas in Laguna Beach, a fancy restaurant.

As I hand her my membership card, she touches my hand. I have goose bumps. I've waited so long for this moment. She whispers, **"I have a beautiful friend about your age, why don't you call her?"**

Shot and hit, smushed and crushed, body slammed--that's how I feel. What a downer. Now it's confirmed what I've known all along, Spritzer and I aren't going to go out. She just sealed our fate.

I accept her friend's phone number. Maybe, someday in the next six months, I'll call. But only after I get over losing Spritzer. Guess I never really had her.

That night, I make the phone call. Twenty four hours later we go out--Tom and Betsy. A blind date. At her front door, neither of us do back flips.

I'm thinking, "Where is the nearest bar we can go, have our token drink, and get this over with?"

Betsy's probably thinking, "Wait till I get my hands on that Spritzer."

We're both thinking, "When a friend says a prospective date is beautiful, the friend means a beautiful heart."

We go to the harbor. Betsy orders a Cuervo Tequila and Coke; I a screwdriver. We tap dance through small talk. In 15 minutes, Betsy says, "I have an early day tomorrow, better take me home."

The next time in Price Club Spritzer says, "You never called my friend back, she liked you." Since Betsy was so taken by me, I decide to give her another chance. I call. She says, "Sorry, I'm seeing someone. Try again in a month or so."

"Try again?" What does she think this is, a radio call-in contest? On some days, I just don't understand women. Of any age.

# Reader Comments and Tom's Responses

Janet: "Your column ended with, 'On some days I just don't understand women. Of any age.' On what days do you understand women?" Response: *Now that you mention it...*

Anonymous Woman: "Regarding dating older men. I'm 31, he's 47. We get along. I'm no be-bop babe. Why will it end? Not because of money, but I want to be married and have children. He's done all that. Response: *People dating widely apart in age usually have different priorities. That can end the relationship.*

Judie: "I met a wonderful boyfriend at church. You should give that a try." Response: *Hopefully, some of our readers will follow your suggestion. But not just to meet someone.*

## Column 13

# TAKING A NEW DATING DIRECTION

It's time for a new start.  Put the rejections behind me.  Cast aside the blind dates.  Forget the bar scene.  Stop trying so hard.

My friends, Tommy and Bruce, have been asking me to go country and western dancing for months.  I told them square dancing is not for me.  "No," they insist, two-stepping and line dancing are the craze now.

It's another Friday night.  I have nothing to do.  I am not sitting home again.  I've been forced into a country and western dancing corner.

In my closet, I find an old pair of jeans and grab the shirt which looks the most country.  I don't have cowboy boots so a pair of loafers will have to do.  My stomach has the jitters.  I can't believe I'm going out there on my own.  I know absolutely nothing about country dancing.

A cowgirl collects $5 at the door.  Inside, my skepticism turns to optimism--the place is packed with people of all sizes, shapes and ages, dressed in western garb.  It looks like a rodeo.  If only I could dance.

**"Beginners two-step lesson is next,"**  I hear announced.  I'm petrified.  I know I must get out there.  So soon though?  So fast?  No way, I'll watch from the bar.

# MIDDLE AGED AND DATING AGAIN

**"We need more men,"** I hear Rolene, the friendly dance instructor announce. She points at me, **"Come on sir, help us out."**

**"HELP US OUT? ME?** I haven't been on a dance floor in 10 years. Out of the blue a woman takes my hand, "Be my partner," she says. It's the first time in a month a woman has asked me for anything except a chicken salad sandwich or a fruit smoothie. In an instant, we are under bright lights.

I look at her and say, "I apologize. This is my first time ever." "Mine too," she replies. We sound like a couple of virgins.

"Quick, quick, slow, slow," Rolene commands. Unbelievably, our feet are actually moving. Without music, we are two-stepping. I hope we aren't being televised on the Nashville Network. Just when we're kind of getting the hang of it, Rolene ups the pressure, "Now we'll go a little faster, and we'll dance to music."

My partner's toes are getting pulverized. My underarms are soaking wet. Everything's blurry except my feet, but Rolene yells at us not to look down there. Our heads are bobbing alternately-- we're out of sync. This is all happening too fast. I promise myself to take lessons.

Each time around the floor I notice a pretty nisei woman's eyes are fixed on me. I can't imagine why. Then the lesson is over. I'm proud for getting out there. I'm unsure, but I think I'm having fun.

Time passes. I gather the courage to approach the nisei woman who'd been watching me. Maybe she'll remember watching me, maybe not. Maybe she's 30, maybe not.

Right now, her age doesn't matter. She's the only port in the storm. Before I can speak, she's dragging me toward the dance floor. "But," I start to protest. A petite perfumed hand covers my mouth.

"I'm Denise," she shouts. "Denise, I can't dance." "Yes you can. I saw you. Besides, it's new to me also." Somehow we make it around the floor. She's hootin' and hollerin' to the music, having the time of her life.

We're out of step, and she could care less. A blue work shirt is tied off above her belly button. We dance on and off that evening. Men take her away all night, but she returns next to me. Maybe, I'm her father figure. "Let's go dancing sometime," Denise says, as another cowboy takes her away.

I ask someone else to dance. When I return to the rail in front of the bar, Denise is gone. I panic. I run to the parking lot. She's walking to her car.

I yell, "Denise," I was just leaving myself." I wasn't. "How can we go dancing sometime if I don't have your number?" I hand her one of my deli business cards. She looks at the card, "I know your place. It's on Pacific Coast Highway. You serve carrot juice. I'll call you." She avoids giving me her phone number.

Just like that, the new love of my life is gone. Thank God for that carrot juice sign on the sidewalk in front of the deli.

What fun I had tonight. I enjoy most of the music even though my ears are ringing. I have renewed hope. I've found a place to meet nice women.

The dance hall can be intimidating. It's not for the shy or meek. One has to be aggressive and going alone there is a brave act. Still, I'll go back often. Maybe next time with my friends Tommy and Bruce. And, I'll await Denise's call.

## Reader Comments and Tom's Responses

Cookie: "If I were you, Tom, I'd head on down to Leisure World and pick yourself out a wealthy older lady with furniture and a nice house. Move in. Enjoy her Mercedes:" Response: *I could never date a woman for her money. However, if you have any of those Leisure World telephone numbers, leave them on my voice mail.*"

Bill: "Did your country and western lady, Denise, ever call you?" Response: *Not yet. I hope she does. I'm probably too old for her, but she is a beauty with enthusiasm to burn.*

John: "There's finally light for you at the end of the tunnel, that's not from a train." Response: *There is?*

Note from Tom: *Timing is everything. I just bought a new wardrobe. In the mail this week, I received an invitation to join a nudist group. Guess I'll have to decline the invitation.*

## Column 14

# JOHNNY CASH--TOM'S OLD FRIEND PERFORMS

I had one of those pleasant experiences last Friday night which made me feel I'm back to normal after nine months of separation and divorce. The timing was perfect to provide a shot in the arm.

Old friends came to town. Johnny Cash and his wife June Carter performed at the Cerritos Center for the Performing Arts.

Lou Robin, Johnny's manager for over 20 years, has been a pal of mine for almost that long. Last Wednesday, Lou said, "We'd love to have you come Friday night, Johnny is always happy to see you." I took a date.

I first became associated with Johnny in 1976. I was marketing director for the railroad-boxcar themed restaurant chain, Victoria Station. Because Johnny sang train songs, we hired him to do our commercials.

We co-produced an album together. I traveled with him, attended recording sessions, and took in 25 of his concerts. I got to know this man who always performs in black. He's one of the warmest, most gracious people I've ever met. His wife June is a positive influence on him--a granite of strength, a woman above the rest.

In 1977, I went behind the walls of San Quentin prison when he performed for inmates. Some people think Johnny Cash did time in prison. The only time he's spent in prison is to entertain.

# MIDDLE AGED AND DATING AGAIN

Johnny has always shared an empathy with prisoners. The night after that concert, Johnny was doing a television show at NBC studios in Los Angeles. The show was interrupted by a telephone call from a prisoner named Gary Gilmore in Utah. Gilmore's last request was that Cash sing him a song. Cash did, over the phone.

Later that night, Cash was solemn, deep in thought. Yet, as I was leaving, he took me aside, placed his arm on my shoulder and said, "Son, thanks for being with me this week-end. It meant a lot." That's the kind of man he is. The next morning, Gilmore was executed.

Last Friday night, 17 years later, back stage before the show, he approached us. His presence fills the room. He's sold over 50 million records. And yet this humble and gentle giant extends an iron handshake, a warm smile.

"Good to see you Tom." He hugs my date and poses for photos. He's relaxed, in control, and has that Cash twinkle in his eyes. His wife June greets us warmly. I feel lucky to have known them.

Cash's 5-piece band takes the stage. "Folsom Prison Blues" is his first song. Then, "Ring of Fire," "I Walk the Line," and other hits follow.

Next, the real test of a singer. His band leaves the stage. It's just John sitting on a stool with a guitar. He performs several songs from his new album, a collection of songs which highlight one of the most powerful, magnificent voices in the history of singing. His voice will never be duplicated. No other living entertainer belongs to the Songwriter's, Country Music, and Rock and Roll Halls of Fame.

The two hour show goes by in a flash. For me, it's reaching back and touching the past, like going to a high school reunion where a friend who meant a lot is rediscovered.

After a tumultuous year of divorce proceedings, I'm feeling better. Thanks partly to an old friend.

## Reader Comments and Tom's Responses

Rachel: "Johnny Cash is a legend." Response: *You'll get no argument from me. I feel lucky to have known him for so many years.*

Patti: "I want a conversation with someone who remembers what a 78-rpm phonograph record was." Response: *I'll bet Johnny Cash remembers, but sorry, he's taken.*

Kathleen: "You are a gemstone in a pile of rocks." Response: *Is that a kind way of saying I'm a headstone in a graveyard?*

Tom Blake with Johnny Cash in 1976

## Column 15

# SURVIVING THE FIRST YEAR HOLIDAYS

Holidays seem to be particularly tough on people not in a relationship. As a newly separated, middle-aged person, the major holidays the first year weren't exactly memorable.

**New Year's Day**--separated one week. I had no where to go. I like football, but I can't even remember what college teams played in the bowl games. I watched some of the Orange Bowl sitting on a barstool at T.G.I. Friday's. I just wanted someone to talk to. Guess that's what bartenders are for. Somehow, I got through the day.

**Valentine's Day**--seven weeks after separation. Thank God it fell on a Monday so I had to be at work, keeping busy. It would have been much tougher on a Saturday or Sunday, with too much time to think, date night, that sort of thing.

Before leaving the house in the morning, I was listening to the radio. Some couples adopt a song while they are dating. Our song was Berlin's, "Take My Breath Away," featured in the movie, *Top Gun.*

The song comes on. I try to ignore it. Tears began to flow when it hit me there would be no Valentine card from anyone except Mom. I felt alone. Reality struck early enough in the day so I had time to recover. I understood the harshest meaning of the word "empty." Somehow I got through the day.

**Easter**--by then, I had met a woman to date. She invited me to join her and her daughter for dinner at a restaurant. Somebody seemed to care. I squeezed her hand firmly under the table. I was happy to pay.

**July 4th**--bittersweet. My Easter friend and I were having differences. On again, off again. Perhaps I was trying to force a relationship too soon after my separation. We spread out a blanket to watch the fireworks near the jetty in the harbor.

Even though my wife and I had watched the previous July 4ths from points around the harbor, I didn't think about her. I was more troubled over my new relationship. For me, fireworks on the 4th have always been overrated. It's just the American thing to do.

**Labor Day**--sort of a bummer. My Easter friend and I were taking a break from each other. It was the kind of relationship where there are strong feelings and yet you fight all of the time. I'm not a fighter. The chemistry is right but the baggage is wrong. So, Labor Day was pretty lonely.

On the day before, she left one of those, "I miss you" messages on my machine. I caved in and called her back. The same old stuff surfaced. Reminded me of Joan Baez's song, "Diamonds and Rust." I too have already paid. She is in her house; I am in mine, one mile away. I could run there in nine minutes. We didn't get together. The day was a downer. I spent that night at the new Chevy's restaurant sipping a couple of frosty Pacifico beers by myself.

**Forecast for Thanksgiving and Christmas**--at least these should be better than the previous year's versions. Last

Thanksgiving, my wife and I realized our marriage was ending. On Christmas, we parted.

Brutal times. This year I may run off to Mexico, or somewhere else. At the least, I will ensure I'm with friends. Being middle-aged and dating again ain't exactly a Fourth of July picnic.

## Reader Comments and Tom's Responses

Hazel: "For Halloween, why don't you dress up as a middle-aged man trying to date and go out and try to collect some treats?" Response: *Funny, very funny. I'll don a suit of armor and carry a shield.*

Charles: "I'm in the same situation as you. I enjoy your column as do many of my friends. I guess misery loves company. Weren't those holidays just a blast? Response: *We belong to a mighty large company. The only holiday with a blast was July 4th.*

Nancy: "What's your sign?" Response: *I'm a Scorpio— emotional, passionate, and frustrated. I seem to match up best with Pisces, but even that hasn't been working very well.*

## Column 16

# PANCAKES AND SMALL TALK

It's time for my car to be serviced, which is a perfect time to get to know a new woman. When dating again, one needs to take advantage of every dating opportunity. A breakfast blind date is scheduled with a woman who lives near the car dealership. We have been fixed up by a woman friend. Jean and I agree to meet at the International House of Pancakes, the one near the retirement community, Leisure World, at 8 a.m.

Taking reader Steve's advice from a few weeks back, I've scheduled the date early in the day. If Jean cancels, I'll have the whole day to bounce back, and breakfast is one meal I don't mind having by myself.

Jean's "in her 40s," salt and pepper hair, about 5'5" tall. She'll be wearing a red dress with a white scarf--that's what I'm supposed to look for.

Entering IHOP, I discover a single gentleman's paradise. There are a half dozen women waiting for a table or to use the telephone--all with salt and pepper hair. I'm glad Jean mentioned the red dress.

For me, IHOP might be a good place to meet women in 4-5 years. They all seem a little too old for me now. Lots of Leisure World women dine here and they all seem so pleasant.

Jean looks about my age, maybe a year or two younger. **She's not in her 40s.** A teen-age hostess seats us, leaving a regular menu in front of Jean and a senior citizen's menu in front of me.

# MIDDLE AGED AND DATING AGAIN

**"WAIT A MINUTE!"** I silently protest, the hostess made a mistake. Jean quickly has gathered the regular menu in her hands, possibly on purpose so I won't try to grab it. I'm in an awkward position. If I ask to see a regular menu, Jean might think I'm too vain to face being a senior. Worse yet, she might feel I'm implying the menus should have been reversed. I can't win and decide it's best to just live with the situation.

**This is not a big deal.** I'm only insulted a little. I'm not 55 yet, far from it. This has never happened to me. Even with silver hair, I don't look or feel my age. It wasn't as if I walked in here wearing a baseball cap with "Older Than Dirt" or "Leisure World Resident" written on the brim.

Should I cheat by ordering a la senior citizen? Or be honorable by requesting a regular menu? In dating, I've learned, sometimes the truth should go unsaid. I decide I'll try to pass as a senior, the first time ever.

I could get caught. Feelings of guilt get in my way. Guilt can be a very powerful emotion. I've experienced a lot of it over my separation. This is silly. Besides, it's not my fault--I didn't ask for the senior citizen's menu.

My choice is the Senior Rooty Tooty, $2.48--one egg, two bacon or sausage links, and two pancakes with any fruit topping. Waitress Paulette arrives. Jean orders. Paulette turns to me. I ask, "May I get an extra pancake with this item?"

Paulette seems suspicious; she senses fraud. She knows I'm not 55. She has likely seen my type in here often--a senior imitator. She raises an eyebrow and answers, "One dollar more."

"OK," I respond, avoiding eye contact with Paulette and Jean.

I squirm uncomfortably. What if the manager asks for ID? I'll say my wallet, which is in my pocket, is in my car, across the street at the car dealership. The street is busy and dangerous. Would IHOP make a senior citizen risk life and limb just to prove age?

Breakfast is delivered. Paulette remains suspicious. Jean thinks I'm 55, and probably too old for her. She insists on going dutch. Now she likely thinks I'm cheap. My bill is $4.21. Jean excuses herself, mumbling something about a 9:30 a.m. bridge game.

On the way out, I look at a regular menu. I saved $1.39. Paulette is shaking her head. She may feel I should be removed from the streets.

## A Week Later

A week later, I take a date to the movie, "Forrest Gump." At the ticket window, the kid, looking at me, says, "Two seniors?"

**What the hell is going on here?** The second senior citizen inference in a week? Have I suddenly aged? Is single life causing wrinkles? My date quickly answers, "Just one." She's 48, looks 45. There is no way she is buying into the senior bit for her. Before I can protest, the tickets pop through the slot.

I save three bucks. A Mr. Goodbar is two bucks. I remember when they were a nickel. Overall, I saved a buck. The total savings due to senior citizenship for the week: $2.39. It's wasn't worth the pain.

Outside the movie theater, I decide I won't cheat on my age ever again. I'd better get out the Grecian Formula. There are three months remaining before I become a senior citizen. I'll live that time to the fullest.

## Reader Comments and Tom's Responses

Betsy: "You're cheap, you wouldn't pay for Jean's breakfast." Response: *Jean wanted no obligation, she insisted on going dutch. She got the hell out of there as fast as she could.*

Sharon: "You have to be happy with yourself before you can have a relationship and you aren't happy." Response: *I'd rather be unhappy alone than unhappy in a relationship. In due time, the happiness will return. What do you want me to do, be a hermit?*

Eddie: "I had my first date in over a year. Reservations were made at a nice restaurant. I picked her up on time and opened the car door for her. The latter set her off. 'This is the 90's, not the 60's,' she screamed. She kept yapping about women being able to open their own doors. I drove her around the block and terminated the date. Women aren't worth the trouble." Response: *Where did you take her on the second date? Women who don't want to be treated as women had a bad experience somewhere in their past. Don't give up, there are lots of nice women out there.*

## Column 17

# A WEEK-END VISIT WITH
# A SPECIAL LADY

We all need to get away once in a while, leave town, see some new scenery, and enjoy a break. Change helps us to take stock, and to put some different perspective in our life. For me, it's a chance to reflect on a bumpy year, after the separation from my wife.

I drive to Northern California. I have dinner with friends at a delightful place called California Cafe, the flagship restaurant of a budding chain. The restaurant is located a few miles north of the Golden Gate Bridge in Corte Madera, in central Marin County. I tell my friends that I'm on the way to see a special woman I've known for some time.

On Saturday morning, I arrive at her place in Sonoma County. That night, we have dinner at Willowside Cafe, west of Santa Rosa, a quaint 50-year old converted roadhouse, which seats about 40. From their extensive wine list, we select a Pinot Noir from the Carneros region of Sonoma County. My special lady picks up the tab.

We stay at her place near the Kenwood Vineyard, half way between Santa Rosa and the town of Sonoma, in an area called The Valley of the Moon.

My special lady is elegant, knows and understands me well, is tolerant and doesn't criticize. She's always happy to see me and she's big in my heart.

On Sunday, we drive over the mountain to my favorite place in the world, the Napa Valley. The fall colors are starting to appear around the vineyards. The grape harvest is winding down.

We have lunch in St. Helena, at Tra Vigne, a special restaurant. Sometimes reservations must be made 5-6 weeks in advance, especially for week-ends. Raviolis filled with smoked turkey and goat cheese compliment the smell of grapes being crushed at the little Merryvale Winery next door. The setting is romantic. Time is flying by.

On Monday morning, my special lady prepares breakfast and makes some old-fashion type sandwiches for my trip home. A glorious week-end is ending. At 6:54 a.m., I'm out the door for the nine hour drive back to Orange County.

It's always tough to say good-bye to the special lady I've called Mom for 54 years.

## Reader Comments and Tom's Responses

Jason: "Your mom is the best date, correction, 'only date' you've had this year." Response: *That's why I keep going to see her.*

Cindy: "You didn't include your voice mail telephone number last week. Are you depressed?" Response: *Sometimes things just slip through the cracks, that was merely an oversight. Talking to readers isn't depressing, usually.*

Patti: "That was a great tribute to your Mom. I get a kick out of her. She's darling. You two have such good communication." Response: *As you can tell, she is very special to me.*

## Column 18

# A RUN-IN WITH A NASTY LITTLE COWGIRL

After the first night of country and western dancing, I return four times in a week, hoping to see Denise, my first dance partner. She hasn't called or come by the deli for a carrot juice as she promised. I should have known.

Country and western dancing has given me a new place to go and something to do. Lessons are desperately needed. I don't know any line dances comfortably enough to get out there yet.

The only couples dance I've learned besides the beginning two-step is the Desperado Rap. That's fun because it's easy and the man stands behind the woman, holding her hands above her shoulders. It's also the kind of dance where you brush up against each other. My pals Tommy and Bruce don't even know that dance and they think they're pretty hot stuff on the floor.

Denise hasn't returned. I meet Ann Marie, a woman much closer to my age. She asks if I'd be interested in taking private lessons with her, adding: "It's like ESP. Just today I was hoping for a dance partner and you enter my life." I say no because her proposal sounds too confining to me. Besides, she seems like the type who will always be at arm's length and that's not what I'm interested in now. I want someone to hug.

My pals are on my case for not having the proper attire. So I purchase a pair of Dan Post gray boots and a belt to match--$175.

I'm pretty stoked with my new garb. Denise will probably flip over me now, if I ever see her again.

But it's an off night. Some nights are like that. Perhaps it's the nights you don't meet anyone nice for you. Those nights sort of bring you back to earth, making you realize that being middle-aged and dating is a drag and can be very lonely.

At 10:30 p.m., a young cowgirl cutie staggers up to me, wearing a low cup top, displaying a healthly cleavage. She slurs that she's from Oshkosh, or a place like that. She sticks her cigarette in some guy's cocktail while he's on the dance floor. She wants a drink. She's damned good looking, but equally as obnoxious. I take her hand, leading her to a barstool.

"Bartender. Large black coffee."
She protests, "I wants a reeeeeeel drink."
I say, "You're drunk."
"Yurr right, I'mmm drunk."

She tells me she's 23, been married three times, and has a five month-old child. She sounds and looks like a perfect match for me--less than half my age and raising a baby. My mom would box my ears if she saw me now.

She says, "I cann make yuse the best breakfast yuse ever had." I start thinking: AFFAIR. It's been a long time since I've had a fling with a woman, let alone one 32 years younger. Actually, I haven't been with anyone except my estranged wife for nine years.

"When?" I respond, "Tomorrow morning?" My juices are flowing. She misses the point. I try again: "If it's tomorrow morning, it'll have to be early. I open my deli at 10 a.m." I hand her a business card. She buries it deep, between her breasts. "Yuse got dell-ee? Yuse got beagles?" "You mean bagels?" "Beagles. I love beagles. I commin' tomorrow mornin' for a beagle and cream schnees." I picture a dog eating cream cheese. I ask, "Aren't you cooking me breakfast?" "I cann fix you..." "I know. I know." She's making inviting statements, but the conversation's not going anywhere. I see the tip of my business card sticking up from her bra. I switch tactics. "Why don't I drive you home?" Now, I'm assuming the role of a good Samaritan. I'll protect her from having a traffic accident, from hurting or killing herself or anyone else. I'm going out of my way to help her.

She claims she's with friends. We wander back to tell them she's going with me. I can't believe my luck. I hope the condoms in my glovebox haven't turned to dust yet. The guy who had the drink in which she put her cigarette has obtained a fresh cocktail. I'll bet he was furious. Her friends rush to her in a panic. They look at me as if I'm an old pervert. My illusions are dashed.

As they drag her away, she reaches for me, "I'm Sandee Jones. I'm listed. Call mees too-marrow. I want a beagle. Do you have raisin..." As she gets farther away, her lips continue to move but her voice is overpowered by a video of singing group Confederate Railroad performing, "Trashy Women."

Country and western dancing has been good therapy. But there's still lots of rejection. Some women say no when I ask them to dance. Some women never get asked to dance. That's pretty sad. One can be lonely standing at the bar having no one with whom to dance or talk. It's good exercise and fun. It's still better than being alone because there's always hope as new cowgirls pour through the front door.

Denise never returned. Sandy never collected her beagle. I wonder if my business card is still buried in her Grand Canyon? She probably dug it out in the morning and wondered who the asshole was that stuck it down there. Another adventure in the world of dating after marriage ends is over.

## Reader Comments and Tom's Responses

Evelyn: "I'm middle-aged and not dating because there aren't enough nice men around. I love country and western dancing. You are going to the wrong places. Go where people love to dance, not drink. Don't give up. Response: *There aren't enough nice men around? How many do you need?*

Anonymous woman: "You are a jerk. You go after young women. You turned down a lovely woman your own age." Response: *I wasn't ready for the commitment of a full time dance partner. Just because a woman is near my age doesn't mean I have to say yes.*

Anonymous woman: "You are so irritating to me. You're one of those disgusting men who stand at the bar all night and won't move your fanny on to the dance floor." Response: *Wait a minute! I've asked women to dance and they turn me down because I'm not Arthur Murray or Don Juan out there. Why don't you and I meet and we'll trip the light fantastic. More likely, we'll probably just trip.*

## Column 19

# A FOOTBALL TEAM NICKNAMED THE "ARTISTS"

I went to a high school homecoming football game. My date's son plays on the team. I arrived at her home a few minutes late. A little annoyed, she said, "This is the biggest game of the year, a sellout. We might not get in and we'll miss the festivities." I could have said, "You're late everytime we go somewhere, what's the big deal? This isn't Plano, Texas, vs. Ft. Worth Lutheran where they draw 15,000 fans," but I didn't.

I told her if it were necessary, we'd climb the fence and sneak in. But I wasn't sure how I would get her over the fence, she's not very athletic and she's got a pretty big fanny. We hurriedly walked the half mile to the stadium from her home.

As we approached, I could see the scoreboard clock indicating the kickoff was still 9 minutes and 23 seconds away. There were only about 100 people in the stands. 50-yard line seats were still available. Mothers tend to exaggerate when their children are involved.

One feels for this home team--they sort of get killed every week. The school only has 500 students. Tonight's opponent has over 2000. When one considers the band, the cheerleaders, the cross country team, and the kids who help in the snack bar, it's a wonder there are any students left to sit in the stands.

# MIDDLE AGED AND DATING AGAIN

On the first play of the game, the opponent, University High, gained 43 yards. The parents looked at each other as if to groan, "Here we go again." Last week, the home team lost 56-14.

The school's nickname is **The Artists**--as in painters and sculptors--not exactly a name to strike the fear into the hearts of Titans, Lions, or Tigers.

The team fought valiantly against University, holding them scoreless in the second half. Of course, University scored 34 points in the first half. Still, the coach could declare a moral victory for the second half. These kids have a spirit which is important in this country. Outmanned, they don't give up.

By halftime, there were 2000 crammed into the stands. Festivities commenced with the homecoming parade, which consisted only of four flatbed trucks, donated for the evening by local businesses. Each high school class decorated a truck in a Halloween theme.

One couple's daughter, I was told by my date, was going to be fired from a cannon perched on a truckbed. When the truck drove past the stands, the daughter was inside the cannon, hanging out the muzzle, waving. I couldn't comprehend that she was going to be catapulted into the dark, ocean air. She wasn't, she just rode in the cannon. Her parents were so proud.

When the class of 1998 float went by, I gasped, It seems not so long ago when my class of '57 was the talk of my hometown. God bless these kids, they're facing a tougher world than we faced. Too many temptations, not enough supervision. They've grown up fast. So soon, too soon.

# MIDDLE AGED AND DATING AGAIN

Halftime ceremonies honored members of the 1934 football team. Six of them took the field. Wow, those guys played 60 years ago.

Then the big event--the crowning of the queen. To find out the winner, a magician performed a magic trick on the 50-yard line on the field. From a small fire he started, a bouquet of flowers popped up with the winner's name attached. Cornball, wonderful stuff. Later, the magician told me he'd been nervous, he'd never done that trick before--guess we all want to perform well, regardless of our pursuit.

My date kept asking, "Are you bored?" I wasn't, but I think she was. "No," I answered, "this is what being middle-aged and dating is all about. I don't have to be country and western dancing every night."

After University scored its fourth touchdown, it seemed The Artists' players on the bench hid from the coach so they wouldn't have to go into the game.

Here, game outcomes don't matter. Parents reassure each other as they exit the stadium, "The kids played hard tonight."

After the game, a bunch of us middle-agers spilled on down to the local pub for a well deserved adult beverage. Over a white zinfandel, my date asked, "Did you see my son make that tackle in the 4th quarter?"

"Yea, he was great," I replied, pretty certain that he had never gotten into the game.

## Readers Comments and Tom's Responses

Bill: "My brother plays for The Artists. After the University defeat, they were awesome in winning their final game of the season. Guess you made them mad or inspired them." Response: *Yes. They probably won one for Michelangelo.*

Irene: "It's nice you were able to write about something other than your dating rejections. That was a refreshing column." Response: *Thanks. Getting dumped all of the time gets old.*

My Mom: "When you write about other things besides just dating, it shows your readers that you don't have a one-track mind." Response: *Only she can say something like that and get away with it."*

The woman in the homecoming cannon: "My parents were upset I wasn't shot to the moon. I was just glad I wasn't used as The Artists' secret field goal weapon." Response: *The Artists could have used you and the entire Marine contingent from Camp Pendleton.*

## Column 20

# DUFFY GETS DUMPED

Duffy is the nickname of my friend. He's very likeable, one of the nicest human beings I've ever known.

He's laid back. There's not a mean bone in his body. In athletics, he's known as a tiger, a fierce competitor. He owns his own business. Women think Duffy's "darling."

He's a good looking guy who smiles a lot, and has a warm sense of humor. In his high school yearbook, "Most Sincere" is probably the caption under his name. For a woman, he'd be a prize catch.

He's not dating, but he should be. Duffy's been in a relationship for three years. It's been one of those stormy, "She can treat me like dirt, but I love her anyway" relationships. He's a patient, tolerant person. Instead of moving on, which he'd be wise to do, he has hung around, trying to make it work. He's more than in love with her, he's addicted to her.

They lived together. Then, a few months back, she decides she's moving to New Zealand to work. He gets upset and the relationship gets bumpy. He moves out. They don't see each other for awhile. Then they do. He's a ping pong ball--back and forth, emotions in, emotions out. Times are turbulent. There are a lot of S-curves on their road.

As time winds down for her to leave, he admits to friends her going away is best. He knows it will only be for a year--he'll wait for her. He hopes, by then, he'll have his feelings for her more under control. Maybe, she'll invite him to visit down under. He hopes they will reunite. When she steps back on U.S. soil, he'll meet her, a dozen sweetheart roses in his arms. It will have been the longest of years.

Shortly before she goes, she announces maybe she'll stay instead for two years. She seems to enjoy hurting him.

Perhaps if Duffy had taken a tougher stance with her, had not been so available, had played it cooler, she would have viewed the relationship differently. He needed to take a mean pill. But then, he wouldn't have been acting naturally, which is no good either.

Sometimes a person can be too much in love--the mate chews 'em up. That's sort of a sad commentary on relationships but it's true.

Duffy and his foreign-bound woman spend some special last moments together. For him, it's torture. Finally, she's gone. His heart is empty and torn apart. The next day, her father calls to tell him she arrived safely. To try to make him feel better, his friends remind him she didn't appreciate him. He understands, but it doesn't seem to matter.

After a week, he receives a postcard. She's settled in Auckland, likes it, and *misses him*. He's encouraged. The mailbox becomes his daily hope and his daily letdown. He's like a toothpick, floating aimlessly in Lake Superior.

A month goes by. He's offered a blind date with a very special woman. "I'm not ready," he replies. He's walking around in a daze, sad, and missing her. He confides to friends, "Maybe I'm just wasting my time waiting for her." We think his words are signs of healing.

A week later, a letter arrives, postmarked Christchurch. He rips it open. "Dearest Duffy, I felt it only fair to tell you I've met someone...We will be moving in together..." Tears return to already tired eyes.

He asks: "How could she do that after three years? So soon? It hurts to picture her with someone else." A wonderful person is devastated. Confused. And angry. Often, men take heartbreak harder than woman.

Duffy's going to be OK. He'll be back on his feet someday. He'll have some scars, but he'll be stronger for the experience.

And somewhere in Southern California, there is a woman who will love and appreciate him because he's worthy of it. She'll marvel at her fortune. Then, he will understand that some things are just meant to be.

## Reader Comments and Tom's Responses

Patti: "What a nice caring column about your friend Duffy. He'll be fine." Response: *Duffy is ready to venture out on his first date since she left. He's doing better already, but it will take some time for him to heal.*

Louella: "You portray women as dogs because of all of the rejection. If I was writing a column, I would portray men as dogs for the same reason. Your column gives me an eyeview of men around here. I'm not disappointed yet. Keep your chin up. Someone is for you." Response: *I had a date the other night. She told me her nickname was Fido. Do you think she was putting me on?*

Susan: "Your column has helped me a lot." Response: *There are many of us in the same situation. Writing the column has helped me. I'm glad it's helping others.*

Jake: "You are right, men can become addicted to women. I wonder why?" Response: *Maybe it has to do with that movie,"The Scent of a Woman," or, other obvious points.*

## Column 21

# SOME THOUGHTS ON MIDDLE AGED DATING

### Staying in a "not right" relationship

To go or to stay?   Sometimes we remain in a "not right" relationship too long.   Duffy, in last week's column, was a good example.

What's not right?   It could be any number of things.   Maybe we like them lots.   They like us less.   We want a commitment.   They won't give us one.   We hold on because there is hope.

Or, maybe the relationship or marriage has just plain soured. Whatever our reason for staying, we think someday our mate will change.   Sure, he'll learn to put the toilet seat down, replace the toothpaste cap, screw the cap back on the aspirin bottle.   But, for the most part, people don't change on the big stuff.

So the years go by.   We're afraid to bust out.   We ask for a commitment for the umpteenth time.   They've heard it before and they feel pressured.   They get upset.   Nobody talks for a couple of weeks.   The cycle starts over.   We rationalize again.   It's easier to stay put than to break away.

Is the prospect of being alone worse than staying where it's not right?   For some the risk of leaving is too great.   They never will. They are resigned to a half life.

# MIDDLE AGED AND DATING AGAIN

It takes guts to move on--possibly the hardest decision of one's life. If we go, there likely will be a long and lonely time ahead. It's hard to believe that someday we'll emerge better off, happier.

The consequences of leaving might be too bleak, maybe we'd be wiser staying. What happens if no one else enters our life? Can we handle picturing our partner with someone else?

Waylon Jennings, in his beautiful song, "Dreaming My Dreams," sings about putting beliefs over love. That's a gutsy position, principle over passion. Waylon, don't walk away hoping you'll hear your wife Jesse's voice begging you to stay. This isn't the movies. When you go, you might as well leave the key on the table because the lock is going to get changed.

A friend whispers to you, "Opportunity often comes from adversity." What does that mean, that this emptiness we're feeling will end in happiness? What a blasted confusing time.

Finally, some of us decide to move on. A new person may appear who's crazy about us, who appreciates us, and who actually loves us. That's our hope; timing is everything.

We wonder why we waited so long to leave. We're free, liberated, and keeping busy.

Some folks shouldn't hang around a "not right" relationship too long. Others should. Only those directly involved know the answer.

## The value of advice

New singles get advice from everywhere. When it comes from friends, that's great, it means they care. Of course, they might be wrong. Therapy may be worth the bucks if it makes us feel better and understand.

In the end, we've got to know what's best, what's right for us, and what makes us happy. We must go with our instinct. Use common sense. Try as best we can.

## Where should we go to meet other singles?

On my voice mail, the most frequently asked question is, "Where do I go to meet someone for me?"

Many of us don't know where or how to begin. We're middle-aged, we never thought we'd be alone. One thing is for sure, you won't meet someone sitting on your sofa. **GET OUT OF THE HOUSE!**

The Grisham novel will still be on the coffee table tomorrow night. But Mr. Right won't still be standing in the supermarket line. Get out, pursue activities you enjoy.

Men and women alike need to be bold. Let's say you see someone you'd like to meet. You're afraid to say hello. If you let the opportunity slip by, it's gone forever like an unfilled airplane seat. Women may say, "I wasn't raised that way. I can't ask a man to dance. It's against my nature." Guess what? Being alone and miserable wasn't in our script either. Our generation has been sort of cheated in a way. We've been dealt a hand we didn't expect, and one we aren't prepared to handle.

81

Recently I went to a party. Sixteen middle aged women acquaintances got together. They asked a male friend to round up the same number of men. Very few of us knew anybody so it was a little awkward when first walking in. Was it love all around? Of course not. Maybe a romance or two might emerge. But new friends were made. It sure beat sitting home that night. All agreed we will do it again soon. The key to the successful night: an equal number of men and women.

Remember: **GET OUT OF THE HOUSE!**

## Reader Comments and Tom's Responses

Candy: "I feel really alone. Your column makes me aware there are others like me. My husband and I broke up. I'm 41 and have four children. Because of my bad experience with him, I'm mistrustful of men and afraid to venture out. I'd like to meet a decent guy, but don't know where to go. I don't want to do the bar scene I did in my 20s. I feel like a baby starting out again."
Response: *You need to start by getting out of the house. You may have to be aggressive. If you see someone while shopping or at work you want to meet, introduce yourself. Be careful. Find a woman friend to go with you. Good luck.*

Alexis: "I've been afraid to leave a 'not right' relationship for years. You hit the nail on the head in your column." Response: *Sometimes, it's hard to find the key to the exit door.*

## Column 22

# LIVING THE SPEED LIMIT--TOM'S 55

The countdown to turning 55 is finally over. The day came and went harmlessly, although I needed a hair dryer to blow out so many candles on the cake. Technically, I'm a senior citizen now. I wonder if my Mom will still call me the perennial sophomore?

A birthday card read, "Age isn't so bad. Ugly is what you have to watch out for." How true!

Hitting 55 is like New Year's. One reflects back, not on just the previous year, but on all of the years.

I've been fortunate, I've had my health. There's nothing more important and I try to give thanks for that daily. Some of my friends didn't make 55. Of my 20-member fraternity class of 1961, 18 are living.

Marriages took place in New York City; Tiburon, California; and Santa Ana, California. Each failed, not a good statistic. My birthday found me solo again, but far better off than 11 months ago when the separation occurred.

I'm no longer the new kid on the marriage-in-trouble block. Some friends have subsequently joined this rather undesirable association. The marriage-divorce club is like a back-loaded mutual fund--easy to join but expensive to exit.

Some great cities have been home. I was born in Jackson, Michigan, and schooled in Ann Arbor, Michigan. I have lived in Chicago, New York City, San Diego, San Francisco, Denver, San

Rafael, Laguna Niguel, and now Dana Point. I lived one year in the Nevada desert, four months in Newport, Rhode Island, and four years in the Indiana farmland.

Some exciting companies have been my employer: Goodyear, Irvine Trust Company, the United States Navy, American Airlines, Trans World Airlines, Victoria Station, ABC radio, the Oakland Invaders football team, and a few others. My hope was someday to be a corporate vice president, but I never made it.

A marketing and sales career required extensive travel. Over a million frequent flyer miles were in my account. A few years ago, carrying my bags down Concourse E at O'Hare Airport at 5 p.m. on a Friday for the umpteenth time, trying to get home by midnight, I decided I had had enough of the corporate world.

**I left the big bucks and big ulcers to make big sandwiches.** I opened a deli in Dana Point. There would be no more staff meetings, no more business suits, no more reserved parking spaces, and no more asshole bosses. My plan was to serve lunches for two years, and then sell out. I'm still there after six years. The deli provides a living and a nice lifestyle--shorts and golf shirts year around, no commute, and frequent peeks at the Pacific Ocean. I'm never hungry. The biggest benefit: Having friends come in every day and my loyal employees.

I'm blessed with a close, wonderful family. Two sisters and a brother. Mom's my best friend. Her birthday is the same day as mine.

What's ahead? I hope to live in south Orange County but it's expensive. Somehow, it will work out. We've all seen others move away and then come back. Everything's fine in Taos or Tahoe until two feet of snow falls. It's hard for those folks to accept in mid-February that your weekends are filled with mowing your lawn and going surfing. They long for the ocean and orange Catalina sunsets.

Perhaps some travel? That would be nice. In 1960, I went to Europe for 85 days for $800. Nowadays, that might get you to Rome and back and maybe a pretzel at the airport. A trip to Fresno is probably more likely. Retirement: No way. Can't afford it. Besides, I want to remain vital. A friend told me regarding my writing to keep my day job.

Another woman in my life? God I hope so! I have no interest in going it alone. Middle-aged and dating is a chore, but necessary, at least for me. Who knows, maybe I've already found her? Or her me.

The most important lesson learned: Nurture old friends, they are irreplaceable. So far, 55 feels good.

## Reader Comments and Tom's Responses

Carol: I adore you and your column. We're living in the best place in the world. I was born here but moved away for 23 years to Salt Lake City, Denver, and Kansas City. I came back three years ago. I hope I never have to leave again." Response: *We must speak softly, we don't want all of those out of state folks invading our land.*

Damion: "At least you've lived an exciting life." Response: *I've been lucky and willing to try new things. Success can't always be measured by success because heaven knows I've failed often.*

Blue-eyed blonde: "I'm amused. You just want to fill up several black books." Response: *You didn't help. You didn't leave your name and number. Blue is my favorite color.*

## Column 23

# RUNNING WITH THE TURKEYS

The second largest Thanksgiving Day race in the United States draws 4,000 runners to Dana Point, California, on Thanksgiving morning.

Being an ex-cross country runner, normally I would run in the 10k race. But a woman friend I date wanted to run so we opted for the 5k. She probably hadn't run over a quarter mile at one time in her life.

We didn't carb-up on pasta the night before. In fact, I probably carbed-down by having a couple glasses of wine to help me fall asleep.

My unmentioned goal for her was that she complete the three miles in 36 minutes. A 12 minute mile is reasonable and finishing last was unacceptable. What a festive event. Runners in this neck of the woods are missing out if they don't run in the Turkey Trot.

Immediately apparent is the variety of attendees--young, old, handicapped, women, men, kids, dogs, you name it. Most are dressed in jogging type clothes with shirts that read USC (of course), UCLA (of course), Notre Dame (I suppose, inevitable), Iowa, Ball State (that's in Muncie, Indiana), Green Bay Packers and Georgia Tech. Those of us living out here come from all over.

# MIDDLE AGED AND DATING AGAIN

One woman ran dressed as a turkey, bird legs and all. A group of nine were tied together as Santa's reindeers with bells and red hats. Another woman went the entire race on crutches. When we realized she only had one leg, it brought goose bumps. She deserves an award for the most inspirational. She finished in front of us.

Dogs are a big deal. Lots of golden retrievers and laos. There were a couple of whippets wearing blankets and two Brittany spaniels. The neatest dogs--a pair of huge Newfoundland's who finished in front of us.

My dog ran. While waiting for the race to start, a stranger petted here from behing. She snapped at him. I turned to apologize and about fell over--the guy was my pal Foxy. We ran cross country together at DePauw University in Greencastle, Indiana, 37 years ago.

During the run, a harbor full of boats and the blue ocean are seen on one side and the Dana Point cliffs on the other. A seal was frolicking behind the breakwater, and a sea gull was perched on the head of writer Richard Henry Dana's statue.

Because this was my woman friend's first race ever, we were cruising toward the rear. Back there, I heard conversations such as: "What time are you putting the turkey in the oven?" and "I bought this incredible pink dress for a cocktail party." At least they have their priorities straight. I encouraged my friend to try to stay ahead of two baby strollers being pushed by a couple of dads.

Dana Point's David Ashford ran. He's our hope for the hurdles in the 1996 Olympics. Before the race, one guy jokingly said to

David, "Runners with less than one percent body fat aren't allowed." When the starter's pistol sounded, David was gone in a flash.

The most touching moment--a 6-year old named John who had finished the race on roller blades got separated from his mother. Tears of fear poured from young eyes, a tiny tot lost in a maze of mingling bodies. I've never seen anyone so frightened. Joan took him by the hand to the public address announcer. The hearts of all of us standing nearby went out for this special child. When his mama finally showed, there were no dry eyes around the podium.

The most lasting impression: the sense of community and camaraderie generated by this event. Our small city should be proud.

As for us, we fell short of our 36 minute goal. It took 45 to be exact. A bride moves faster down the aisle. But as we walked toward the car, my friend said, "Next year I plan to run the 10k." Mission accomplished, she was hooked. While the baby strollers beat us, we didn't finish last.

# Reader Comments and Tom's Responses

Rod: "I'm a former divorced guy. My wife and I go out on dates to keep the romance alive. I like your comments on local events like the Turkey Trot." Response: *Married or single, folks need to get out of the house to put a little spice in life.*

Maxine: "I feel anxious reading your columns, short of breath and frenzied. You are moving too fast and in all directions. You're trying too hard and too soon." Response: *You'd be out of breath if you ran three miles also. Regardless of what one does to recover from a divorce, time is the biggest healer. How one fills that time is another issue. I elect to get out there, to try, to fail, to pick myself up, and get going again.*

## Column 24

# WAS SHE REALLY THE PRESIDENT'S SECRETARY?

Country and western dancing is becoming more comfortable for this middle aged and dating guy. Three line dances have been learned. I purchased an instructional video for a dance called the *Boot Scootin' Boogie*, because it's danced often at the club where I go. I've spent hours watching that video, mastering the dance.

For the first time ever country dancing, I'm looking forward to the disc jockey's words, "Get on the floor all you boot scooters." I can now do the dance blindfolded. I know it cold and am brimming with confidence. Now I can be one of those cool guys who knows all of the steps and doesn't have to keep looking at the feet of others who know the dances. I laugh, thinking maybe the management here will ask me to be an instructor.

Finally, the big moment arrives. *My* boot scootin' boogie is next. As the music starts, I've got a giant grin on my face. I'm revving my engine like one of those funny-car drag racers. Then, something goes wrong. Holy horrors! The disc jockey must have made a mistake. I'm doing a different dance than everyone else on the floor.

I'm making an ass of myself. I feel like Tom Hanks in the movie Apollo 13, "Houston, we have a problem." I crawl to the rail and disappear into the noncaring crowd. What the hell happened?

I seek out dance instructor Rolene. She informs me there are eleven different versions of Boot Scootin' Boogie. I learned the Texas version, not the California one, which is taught here at the CRC. All that time wasted. Why did Blockbuster Video sell a Texas version of Boot Scootin' Boogie in California? This middle aged and dating gentleman has suffered a minor setback in his quest to find a mate.

I can two-step forward pretty well. Two-stepping backward is still awkward even though I've practiced backward around my kitchen floor over 200 times. When my dog sees me moving in reverse, she tilts her head, puzzled. She moves backward more fluidly than I.

The waltz is not a difficult dance. I get messed up going from the waltz beat back to the two-step beat. Dancing comes easy to some folks, I'm not one of them.

On a Saturday night, two weeks after being with the drunken 23 year-old cutie, I'm having another off night. But that's OK, my expectations aren't as high. I haven't even two-stepped yet; I've just done a few line dances. There has been no woman in my arms. Too many couples and too few singles are here on Saturday night.

A mid to late-40ish woman is standing next to me. I haven't paid much attention to her. We're watching the maze of dancers go around. No one has asked her to dance. We begin to make small talk. Her English accent is cute.

Jennifer's her name, she's been in this country from Australia for 20 years. We dance often, she is patient with my jerky style. The more I'm with her, the more I like her. She's charming, confident, and has **devilish eyes**. I realize that earlier in the night, I had made a middle aged dating mistake--I had judged her before getting to know her. When I first saw her, I thought she wasn't pretty enough or her body wasn't shaped the way I'd like it to be. In the restroom. I looked in the mirror. I realized she probably was thinking the same type of thoughts about me.

Jennifer tells me she's the secretary to the president of Taco Bell. I'm impressed. I visualize going to cocktail parties with a feisty Aussie on my arm, saying, "This is my girlfriend, Jennifer. She's the secretary to the president of Taco Bell." I picture hundreds of free tacos to eat. I decide I'd like to pursue this woman. And I've only had one glass of wine.

It's Saturday night, she's alone, wearing no wedding ring, and is friendly. I work up the courage to tell her I enjoy her. Nothing too heavy. She's the first woman semi-near my age who's had an affect on me. Maybe I'm wrong, or maybe it's just the way I feel, but there seems to be some chemistry between us. I haven't felt this way in a long time.

At 11 p.m., she abruptly says, "Good night." There was no lead-up-to conversation like, "Tomorrow I'm going to church early." Her proclamation surprises me, but I've had enough sales training to handle the objection. "May we have dinner sometime?" is my comeback.

She hesitates before answering, "That will be difficult. There are complications." I ask, "How can I reach you?" She replies, "You may call me at work."

I watch her nice fanny wiggle away. Why, I wondered, does middle aged dating have to be complicated? Here are two nice people together on a Saturday night, why can't we go grab a cup of coffee? She definitely had a change of heart, it wasn't as if I tried to kiss her or anything like that. I'm puzzled, what does Jennifer mean by, "There are complications?" Don't be naive, Blake, her statement probably means she's in a relationship. Maybe her boyfriend or husband is away on a business trip. I'm prepared for that. But why was she here on a Saturday night alone and why did she seem so friendly earlier? I wonder, do women really come here just to dance?

Unwilling to give up easily, I decide to follow up, to call her at Taco Bell. Is she really the secretary to the president? Being middle aged and single and having to play it cool seems so silly. Still, I don't call her until Tuesday, all of two days.

"Are the complications surmountable?" I ask her over the president's alternate phone line. "At this point, no they aren't. Maybe we'll see each dancing sometime. Good-bye."

That's it, she ends the conversation. When one calls the president's secretary, one best be quick with personal business. Chalk up another attempt at dating a nice woman. Rejection. It's kind of discouraging. I think maybe I should stop going to the CRC. At least she was the president's secretary.

Taking Jennifer out would have been nice. At least I now know that someone near my age can get my heart started. That's an important revelation for me. Thoughts of having fun with her haunt me for a few days, but I decide it's best to forget her. I think if she had gone out with me she would have had a good time. But she doesn't know that. She probably categorized me as just another horny middle-ager. Which, of course, I'm not.

A month later, I see Jennifer at the CRC. Admittedly, I'm excited to see her but she's not as intriguing as before. On the dancefloor she admits her life isn't complicated after all. She felt I was being too forward the night we met so she fabricated the "complications" story.

"Too forward? Because I said I enjoyed your company?" I said. She shrugged her shoulders. I decided the problem was hers, not mine. I'd just like to find a nice women I can date and be with for more than one or two times. At least, Jennifer's excuse was original. I'd never heard the "complications" excuse before.

I've decided not to pursue her. Timing's everything--we probably missed our timing crossroads by a month. I doubt if she'll lose any sleep over my decision. Country and western dancing is complicated enough. Why does life also have to be? How about a waltz, Matilda?

## Reader Comments and Tom's Responses

John: "You started writing your column about the time my wife of 23 years left me. I hope you find someone. Me too, hopefully my wife. A group of men whose wives dumped us meet every Tuesday at 6 p.m. at Coco's restaurant in Mission Viejo. Why don't you join us? We have fun." Response: *If I were a middle aged woman looking to meet a gentleman, I'd show up at Coco's.*

Geri: "It's refreshing to hear about a man who is aggressive, forward, and has the gumption to meet a lady. I'm middle aged and dating. You are a doing a tremendous service for your community and perhaps our entire planet." Response: *Come on Geri, perhaps a few folks around the neighborhood, but not the entire planet.*

Linda: "You're a great looking guy, but your eyewear is passé. Get a new pair." Response: *Ah ha, that's my third order of business. The first is to get a date. The second is to darken my hair.*

## Column 25

# LIVING LIKE HOBOS

In the song, "King of the Road," Roger Miller sang of hobos who couldn't afford rent, phones, a pool or even a cigarette. Was Miller singing about conditions in the 70s or in Orange County, California, in late 1994? Nearly every new middle-aged single is affected by a common thread, a different and usually more difficult, living situation.

I'm talking about shelter, the roof over our heads. When couples separate, the cost of shelter increases. Instead of one living cost payment, now there are two. Ouch! The pinch begins.

Most of us in Orange County have felt the real estate slump of the last few years. Take me, for example. It's hard to fathom that just over four years ago my wife and I **stood in a lottery line** with 300 other potential buyers to pay top dollar for a home with a view of the Pacific Ocean. May I repeat that? I stood in a lottery line.

We gladly agreed to a 11 percent fixed mortgage. We figured by now our house would have increased fifteen percent or more. That's how California real estate had always performed for me.

Three years later, to save money, as so many others did, we refinanced to an adjustable rate mortgage. The house's value has decreased fifteen percent--a $105,000 swing. Equity around here is just a six letter word.

I accepted the house in the divorce settlement. Foolish me, I should have made my wife suffer with me through the question of

97

what to do with the house. But, we wanted a clean break so I agreed to keep it.

This March, the adjustable goes from 6.5% to 8.5% or $433 per month, that's a hell of a hit on one income. What to do now? Take a roommate to offset the cost? At my age, a senior citizen, bringing a stranger into my house? Don't think so--I've heard too many ugly roommate war stories.

One friend took in a roommate, a guy who said he'd seldom be home because he worked so much. Once the guy moved in, he seldom left. He was drunk some of the time. Twice he left pots on the burner after passing out, several times red wine found the carpet, and pizza was on the couch. Not exactly a delightful arrangement.

Another pal's roommate befriended an older, religious woman who lived next door. The roommate told the woman he'd go to church with her to meet some of the singles at her church. She believed she was saving a soul. At 10:00 a.m. one Sunday, she knocked on the door, dressed in her Sunday best, "Tell Jerry it's time to leave for church."

My friend found it awkward to explain that his roommate was still asleep--with the woman he'd been shacked up and drinking with for two days. The neighbor woman was crushed.

Two of my deli customers live together as friends, not lovers. He calls her "the geek magnet" and she calls him "the chick repellent." Actually, they're fortunate, they get along well.

Having a roommate is like owning a bed and breakfast inn. A stranger's often in your kitchen at odd hours. There is always someone's car in the garage and guests' showers seem to last forever. Why do landlords always know, and tenants never know, when the first of the month is?

So the roommate arrangement is out. Maybe it's time to sell the house, to downsize as so many corporations are doing. The only problem is there are seven homes for sale on my street, and it's a short street. Also, half of them will be a short sale. I guess I can live in an apartment after owning my own home for 22 years, but I'd prefer not to.

To me, foreclosure always happened to some joker who couldn't manage his money. With pink slips falling like rain in Orange County, it's now within the realm of possibility for many of us. An executive who lives down the street lost his job. Now he's mowing lawns just to stay afloat until his overpriced home sells. Sad stuff.

That retail sales clerk who impressed you may have an MBA and just last month might have been a vice president in the human resources department of an aerospace firm. Professional basketball players who mope because their eight year contract is worth only $70,000,000 make me sick.

The housing issue is just another one of those cards middle aged singles never planned to be dealt. Not many of us ever thought we'd find ourselves in the positions we're in.

Roger Miller ends his song by claiming he's not King of the Road. I know how he felt.

## Reader Comments and Tom's Responses

Bill: "Re: your article on being stuck with the house. Boy, can I relate. I've been in this place for 3 years hoping for a market recovery. I've decided to put the house on the market and take a $60,000 hit. Bad scene, bad scene. With all of the other problems in this county, I will probably have trouble selling it. I'm going to buy a boat and live on it in either Dana Point or San Diego. By the way, darken your hair, you'll be amazed at the results." Response: *Will darkening my hair help my house sell? Is that what you meant?*

Carol: "Do you ever date women resulting from your column? Response: *My column is not a dating service! That was never the original intent of writing it. There are ethics, professionalism, honor, and commitment to journalism at work here. However, there is this crazy redhead who tracked me down...*

Laney: "Concentrate more on your grammar and less on your escapades." Response: *Both need lots of polishing.*

## Column 26

# WIDOWS GET TREATED DIFFERENTLY

"Would you like to go to a Charles Wysocki art exhibit?" a woman friend recently asked me. "Charles Wysocki? Who's that? Art exhibit? On a football Saturday? Seriously? OK. I'll go."

When one is middle aged and dating, one should be open-minded, willing to try new things, even a little culture. So off we went to Art Works, a gallery in Fountain Valley on Brookhurst.

Wysocki does original paintings, primarily of old New England settings. A limited number of photo offset lithography prints are created, signed and numbered. The printing plates are then destroyed so there will be no further production of prints.

Wysocki has legions of fans. Many of them were standing in line to have their favorite pieces signed by their hero.

My friend's a widow of 19 months. She and her husband collected Wysocki art. Lots of it. They were well known and received at this gallery. Because her husband had been ill, they were often whisked to the front of Wysocki waiting lines. She insists preferential treatment had nothing to do with her husband being a prominent physician or the number of pieces they purchased.

This visit was different. We took our place at the end of the line. After over an hour, it was our turn. Wysocki remembered her. She showed him a list of his pieces she owns. He smiled and simply said, "Thank you for making me rich."

Wysocki is a cherub-faced man who reminds me of W.C. Fields. After four hours of signing artwork, he was cordial and maintained a sense of humor. That impressed me. I can't believe his hand didn't cramp.

But there's more to the story than artwork. This outing was hard on the widow. She and her husband came to these Wysocki exhibits for years. They had what sounds like a perfect marriage. Sharing, caring. He idolized her. A few months after he died she came to a Wysocki showing here and burst into tears. This time she was brave but I could tell she was hurting inside.

The gallery people were happy to see her. "You look wonderful," they told her. I thought they treated her graciously. She felt, however, she was perceived differently. Subtle things she noticed. She wondered if it was because she was no longer married to the prominent physician. Society tends to treat widows and widowers differently, less importantly.

I even felt a bit uneasy. "Is this the doctor's replacement? He does what? Owns a deli? He makes sandwiches?" No one spoke those words, but I sort of felt that way. Maybe, because I was hungry. People get so used to seeing couples together and then something happens, and they don't know how to treat the one who remains. Or the one who remains's escort.

I kept reminding myself that I'm OK, a person, a somebody, a sandwich maker, not just a doctor's replacement.

We left. She was pensive but upbeat. I wondered how she was really feeling inside. Am I like Avis, second best? Will she be able to have a relationship with me or someone else while still being true to her husband's memory? How about me? Could I ever feel she cares for me based on what I have to offer? Thick, heady stuff.

We wanted more punishment. We went to the China Palace in Newport Beach for dinner, a place she and her husband frequented often. "Wait until, you meet Jack the owner, he was always so great to us," she told me. Going there didn't bother me. As I said, I was hungry.

We were seated, but no Jack. Drinks, no Jack. Food delivered, no Jack. Finally, Jack walks by. Joan flags him, "Jack, it's Joan." Jack is tongue tied, obviously surprised to see her without the doctor. He's uncomfortable. He shakes my hand, and does an Oriental bow but his heart wasn't in it.

For her, the atmosphere here is definitely different. It makes her sad. "You see, people do treat me differently."

Before we pay the bill, Jack rallies by sending us a plate of lichee nuts, the ultimate Chinese goodwill gesture. I leave a bigger tip than I normally would. She hopes the old vibes will return if she comes back a few more times.

She mentions some couples stopped seeing her after her husband died. "Women think you're a flirt, even if you aren't. The pain of losing someone is bad enough, treatment like that from former friends makes it so much worse."

We went to her house to sit in front of a fire. Not much was said, but there was lots of thinking. I wondered why I had eaten so many of those disgusting lichee nuts.

# Reader Comments and Tom's Responses

Janet: "I'm appalled you are considering darkening your hair. Why do it? You look smashing with your hair natural. Don't be another older man trying to look younger. It doesn't work. It just makes you look ridiculous." Response: *Yes, you're right. I should quit trying to be like San Antonio Spurs forward Dennis Rodman and more like silver-haired Laker Coach Del Harris.*

Kay: "I'm a handwriting analyst, may I interpret your handwriting? I like your column and read it before any other part of the paper. You sort of let it all hang out. I like your openness." Response: *My penmanship is so bad I print. I feel in order to write for the readers, you need to be deeply personal and honest.*

Maria: "Why is it that middle-aged geezers want to date 20-year olds? There are many very attractive, sexually active, women in their 50s and beyond." *I'm finding dating women closer to my age is what's best for me. Last night I went out with someone only 19 years younger.*

## Column 27

# TAKING A DATE TO SAN FRANCISCO

A guy-thing hobby took me to San Francisco recently. A woman friend tagged along. We've been dating a few weeks.

For 17 years, a group of men have belonged to a fantasy basketball league. We pretend we're NBA owners--we draft players, trade, haggle, argue, point fingers and act immature. Fun stuff. Our season lasts from November until June.

The biggest plus, old friends stay in touch. Draft night is a big deal. There are nine franchises. Awards are presented for the previous season. My favorite: the **Horse's Ass** trophy to the team making the worse trade. A gourmet dinner is served among 13 rounds of selecting players. Forty to fifty hours of preparation time are not unusual per team. Words such as "Dumb pick, good pick" are often heard. Some owners stoop so low as to try to buy drinks for other owners to get them drunk to gain a mental advantage.

My date is being a good sport. She doesn't know anything about basketball, but I've got her crossing out names as players are drafted. She's taking her role seriously, even though she admits she has no idea of what's going on.

In round six, out of the blue, she tells me to select Atlanta Hawk guard Stacey Augmon. I do. So far, he's averaged 21 points for my franchise, unheard of for a sixth-round pick. How did she know he'd do so well? "Simple," she says, "if I'd had a girl, I'd have named her Stacey." Ah, woman's intuition.

Traditionally, a bottle of aged port provided by last season's winner comes out after the final player is picked. Toasts and a few innocuous side bets are made.

After basketball folly, she and I stay at a bed and breakfast inn I had randomly selected from the telephone book. Morningsong, a small ranch house surrounded by seven acres of yellow-leafed grapevines, is located ten minutes from Sonoma's town square. It's a treasure of a place with gracious owners. The husband serves breakfast. He and I discover we both previously worked for restaurant chains. Ironically, he's a good friend of the people we're having dinner with that same night. Small world. Telephone: 707 939-8616. If you're heading toward wine country, give Morningsong a try. About $90.

That night we attend a dinner party at my friend's home in Belvedere in Marin County. I've known him for 30 years. He was a founder of now-derailed restaurant chain Victoria Station. From a spot on their deck, one can see the Golden Gate Bridge, the San Francisco Skyline, the Bay Bridge, and the Richmond-San Rafael Bridge. A two-million dollar view.

After 10" of Marin County rain in 24 hours, we head to San Francisco to spend our last night. Quaint Hotel Griffon got the nod. Located south of Market Street, it's next to the Rincon Annex post office. Bay view rooms look toward Treasure Island. $140. Parking in the area is difficult.

San Francisco is filled with creative restaurants, places that are adapted to keep the historic ambiance of the old buildings in which they're located.

One of these is Gordon Biersch, a restaurant brewery located in the old Hills Brothers Coffee headquarters building. We had lunch watching beer being made and boats going by.

For dinner, my sister suggested another restaurant in a restored building, a new hot spot called LuLu, also south of Market at 4th and Folsom. We tried for a reservation. Amazing--booked until 10:00 p.m. on a Sunday. However, we could eat at the bar so we went.

A wood-burning cook pit is the focal point of the dining room. This is one of those prosciutto-duck confit-persimmon salad kind of places. Reasonable. Packed as promised. Rosanne's Tom Arnold was dining with a young blonde. No one bugged him except maybe she. The limo waiting for them was about a block long.

On Monday, my friend went shopping while I had lunch at the Bohemian Club. Another guy thing, an old buddy's 50th birthday. Later, she and I enjoyed tea in the lobby of the St. Francis Hotel, prior to leaving for the airport.

A nice week-end with a nice lady. I'm feeling better about being single.

## Reader Comments and Tom's Responses

Anonymous woman: "You went to San Francisco for a weekend with a woman you'd been dating only for a few weeks. I'm newly single and concerned. Do you sleep in the same bed or separate beds, after knowing each other for such a short time?" Response: *Years ago, I traveled to Bangor, Maine, with a woman under similar circumstances. She insisted on separate rooms, but there were none available. Then she insisted on separate beds, which turned out to be tiny. When the lights went out, she attacked me. Ever since, I've opted for one king-size bed.*

*A woman has five choices: 1. Sleep on the floor but it's cold down there. 2. Pay for her own room. 3. Occupy the same bed but get as far away as possible. Of course, this position could present problems for her during the night. 4. Bring a box of crackers to bed and spread the crumbs around like laying a mind field. Or, 5, sleep next to the guy. It becomes her decision--whatever makes her happy.*

## Column 28

# FOOTBALL AT THE "HOLLYWOOD" BOWL

Between Xmas and New Year's, I attended the Holiday Bowl at Jack Murphy Stadium in San Diego. College football between Michigan and Colorado State University. Fun stuff.

My sister and her husband, Captain Pete, were along as well as 28-year friends Terry and Billie. And, of course, a date. She wouldn't admit it but I think it was her first college football game ever. She claims to have seen UCLA play once in Pasadena. I doubt it.

Pre-game ceremonies were festive. Our group agreed the Michigan band is one of the finest bunch of marching musicians in the land. "Who doesn't warm to UM's fight song, *The Victors*?" I asked. Terry reminded me Buckeye fans don't.

Navy Leapfrog jumping team members kept dropping out of the darkened sky, often attached in pairs or threes, releasing only at the last second to land their parachutes separately. The crowd was awed. Over the speakers, we heard, "The last chutist is carrying the game ball." Before that chutist landed, we noticed, uncomfortably, another seemed to be having control problems. He was coming in too fast, his chute wouldn't flair.

He landed hard and wrong, on his back. He tried to get up but couldn't. The heretofore entertained crowd was stunned. Now, no one cared about the game ball, only about him. Minutes later he was wheeled away strapped to a gurney. The injury cast a damper on the game, putting what's important in life in perspective. But the show had to go on--65,000 were waiting.

My date is a sweetheart, one of the most gentle people I've ever met. She wanted to know why the word "Rams" was listed under Colorado State's name on the scoreboard. I answered that "Rams" is CSU's nickname.

"I thought the Rams were in Anaheim?" she said, a little confused. I had trouble explaining how there could be two Rams teams in football in Southern California. The Ram mystery became clearer when she saw six CSU students with "Ram Holder" emblazoned on the back of their jackets, holding a live 300-pound ram mascot.

Shifting her eyes across the field, "Where's Michigan's Wolverine?" was her next question. I had trouble explaining that also.

The game began. When Michigan kicked the sickest looking field goal I've ever seen, and I've seen Michigan kick some pretty sick ones, I asked her how many points UM got for that. She held up two newly manicured fingers. I explained a field goal was worth three points. She responded, "Well, in basketball, a field goal's two points." I didn't want to get into the new 3-point basket with her.

She wanted to know what the "1-2-3-4-T-TO" meant across the top of the scoreboard. I told her under each number, she could find each team's score by quarter. And "T" stood for total points and "TO" stood for time-outs remaining. She hesitated, and then softly answered, "That's what I thought."

I encouraged her to watch a few plays through the binoculars I purchased in Hong Kong in 1966 for 20 bucks. "These glasses are so powerful, you'll be able to see the center spit." She said she had no interest in seeing that.

Right in front of us, Michigan had this awesome goal line stand. Eight times CSU tried to score inside the five, Michigan held them. I thought 65,000 pairs of eyes were glued to the action. With those binocs, I knew she'd feel like she was out there, like in the middle of the grunts and the groans, like on the line of scrimmage, in the mud, hearing, feeling, and smelling the intensity, and seeing into the quarterback's eyes.

Wrong. She had the binocs focused on the CSU bench. She whispered to my sister, "Some of those guys have pretty cute fannies." Ah--a woman's love and appreciation for the game of football.

Michigan won 24-14. We enjoyed the night. We pray the chutist recovers from a broken vertebrate. I hugged the New Yorker, the prettiest woman in the stands.

The next day she called her Mother, "Mom, last night we went to the Hollywood Bowl..." When she hung up, I said, "The Hollywood Bowl is where they have outdoor concerts in L.A. We went to the Holiday Bowl." She said softly, "That's what I thought."

## Reader Comments and Tom's Responses

Janet: "I plan to tell the woman's side of middle aged and dating."
Response: *Where? In Playgirl Magazine.*

Beth: "I thought your date was a good sport sitting through that football game." Response: *Yea, especially when she was checking out that football player's behind through the binoculars.*

Joe: "That bit about the Hollywood Bowl was a riot. Did Neil Diamond or Rod Stewart provide the halftime entertainment?" Response: *Naw. I think it was the El Cajon High School marching band.*

## Column 29

# A YEAR OF DATING AGAIN AT MIDDLE AGE

I've heard several people mumble, "I'm glad 1994 is over." I'm one of them.

The year started abruptly. On January 1st, I found myself in a 2/3rds empty house with an AWOL wife. Without telling me, she had decided she'd had enough on XMAS Eve.

Prematurely, perhaps, I soon thrust myself into the middle aged dating world. A storm of protest came from some readers, "You need to heal first." Hogwash, I needed some TLC.

Regardless of age, if a woman wasn't nailed to the floor, I'd ask her out. There was Susie, the Dana Point lass, who agreed to a Saturday date. "I work until early evening, pick me up at 9:30 p.m." A late start was OK with me because I thought maybe it would lead to a late finish.

We went to Brio, a trendy Newport Beach-type Italian restaurant near my home in Dana Point. We sat at the bar. She said she wasn't hungry, but she demolished my calamari appetizer. She said didn't drink, but a white zinfandel in her hand was history before its time. Waiters, bussers and the sauté cook were checking her out. I thought I was Joe Cool. More appetizers and wine were piled on the bar.

Feeling mature, I asked, "What are your goals?" A piece of Octopus flew from her mouth, sticking on the fat part of my

113

wine glass. "I'd like to finish college before I reach age 30," she replied.

While I tried to regroup from her answer, she gathered the errant speck of fish with her forefinger, returning it to her mouth.

I asked, "How soon will you graduate?" She said, "In three years."

If Brio barstools didn't have wide legs, I would have fallen on my ass right there and then. She was 27, I was twice her age.

At 10:40 p.m., apparently satiated, she checked her watch. "It's getting late. I have to go to church early tomorrow. I should go home."

Seventy minutes. That's how long our date lasted. The bill was $35. She cost fifty cents a minute. After that, I stopped asking out young women.

Then along came Captain Combat--my affectionate nickname for her. We were two strong personalities drawn together. George Straight's song, "Easy Come, Easy Go," was appropriate for us, with words something like, 99 times the relationship didn't work. We got along like teeth grinding. We cared lots but who can endure a relationship when your guts are churning half the time?

Enter the Irvine spinster about my age. Potential looked good, her body even better. One night she told me she was having a date with a widower from Sacramento, that she was glad the poor guy's wife had died. I thought my hearing was goofy, but she didn't retract her comment. Up until then, I thought she was a classy woman. I became invisible on the spot, not even her body was worth a comment like that.

As September drew to a close, a New York widow tracked me down. We stumbled through October and November, both dragging lots of baggage. December opened without her, her choice. She said I got my kicks out of spunky, aggressive women, that she was too passive for me. That was the excuse she made, even though she was probably right. I told her I'd paid my dues with those kind of women, that I needed someone like her. I hope it's she.

And so 1994 ends. Datingwise, it's been an adventure. The widow is circling like a confused airplane, unsure of where to land. I've been given more advice than the President.

What I've learned is that being middle aged and dating isn't a stroll through Central Park, or a cruise on the Hudson. Rather, it's like negotiating a mine field. I can't wait to see what's been planted for 1995.

## Reader Comments and Tom's Responses

Norma: "You got what you deserved taking out that younger woman. At 50 cents a minute, she undercharged you because obviously she was bored stiff. Maybe she feels ripped off." Response: *"How could she? She had a double helping of calamari."*

Micholena: "Good grief, get a life. You're wimping along, far too long. Until you put some closure on your unwanted separation behind you, your whining will only attract flies. You are someone, pathetic, left over. You continue to assure your wife she made an excellent exit choice." Response: *"Now I understand what 'cutting to the quick' means. You've got a bee in your butt.*

Bill, Mission Viejo: "You got some adverse comments from women about coloring your hair. Ignore them. Do it anyway. Can't wait to see the new you at the next singles function." Response: *"Now I'm in a quandary."*

Diane: "You've opened my eyes to the guy's side of middle aged dating. You've grown a great deal. Don't forget to look back to see how far you've come. Keep up the good work." Response: *"Experience teaches us well. I don't want to forget 1994, I just don't want to live it again."*

Carolyn: "The more advice you get, the more confused you'll be. I was told not to date for a year after breaking up from a long term relationship because I had baggage. Everyone's got baggage. Should I wait a year?" Response: *"A year? You must be joking. How about a week or however long it takes to dust off your little black book."*

## Column 30

# THE ROSE PARADE IN PASADENA

Readers often ask, "As a middle aged single, what can I do to get out, possibly meet someone, and have fun?" One event which shouldn't be missed is The Rose Parade in Pasadena.

This year, a date and I decided to go. We had no plan other than to head for Pasadena from South Orange County at 6:30 a.m Unsure of where to specifically go, we winged it.

The I-5 to the 57 to the 210 leads into Pasadena from the East. KNX radio announced that the Sierra Madre off ramp was closed and if people weren't already in Pasadena, they should turn around and go home--there was no more room at the big oval inn. We ignored the advice. At 7:30 a.m., we grabbed the exit before Sierra Madre.

"Follow the Goodyear blimp," she suggested. A right, then a left on Foothill lead us to a packed MacDonalds. I needed coffee. She needed a restroom. We needed directions. A customer told us the parade route was a block away, to park where we could and walk.

By 8 a.m., a grassy area, ten feet from where the parade would pass, was secured. People sitting in lawn chairs and perched on step ladders were popping up like mushrooms. The group seated next to us had an open box of donuts. I offered to buy the chocolate one. They said, "Just take it." To boot, they poured us fresh coffee.

Turns out this was a special event for them. The gentleman has a retarded brother living in Wisconsin. The brother had often said if he ever won the lottery his dream was to see the Rose Parade. As a gift, the gentleman had flown his brother out. It was only the brother's second time on an airplane. We got goose bumps watching the reactions of the little man wearing a Green Bay Packers hat, thrilled beyond life.

Just before 10:00 a.m., float number one, a 30-foot tall astronaut passed. We congratulated each other for making the early morning effort to come.

Most courageous parade participants: the Holland, Michigan, High School Marching Dutchman Band, 178 kids who covered the parade route in wooden shoes. A few had shoes missing and were walking in socks. Every so often, they did a high kick routine. Had to hurt. Good for them.

Biggest inspiration: High school bands from all over--Delaware, Nevada, Hawaii, Mississippi, South Carolina, and Osaka, Japan. What a thrill for them. And lots of proud parents.

Most entertaining and talented: The Morris Brown College Marching Band of Atlanta, Georgia. When the parade stopped in front of us, 186 musicians put on a dance routine which was hot, just plain hot.

When the Penn State University band passed, Oregon fans behind us blew their duck calls in protest but were drowned out.

Middle aged dating has changed me. Normally, by 1:30 p.m., I'd be in my seat at the Rose Bowl, awaiting the kickoff. About that time, my date and I were being seated at The Crocodile Cafe, a jammed Old Town Pasadena restaurant. Guess not everybody loves football.

The Rose Parade is a must for those living in Southern California. The beauty of the flowers, the horses, the bands, the people--the enormity of it all. It's a colossal worldwide event. It's close by and it's free.

## Readers Comments and Tom's Responses

Shannon: "You described the Rose Parade beautifully. It's almost a travel guide for folks who have never gone. I'm saving it to use next year." Response: *Anyone who lives within 400 miles of Pasadena should see The Rose Parade in person at least once in their life.*

Dorothy: "I'm not going to The Rose Parade until Northwestern plays Washington State." Response: *You've got a long wait, baby.*

Jack: "You sure get around." Response: *There is lots to do in Southern California.*

## Column 31

# DUMPED BY AN OLDER-YOUNGER WOMAN

A couple of months ago, a message was left on my answering machine, "Tom, I'm a widow of a year and a half. I don't know how to approach this middle aged dating bit. Could we meet some time?"

I agreed. There was something intriguing about her. We started to date. The relationship moved along quickly. She was the aggressor at the start. She was 52, just three years younger than I, the oldest woman I've ever dated. We took a three-day trip to San Francisco. Traveling together tests a relationship. We had a special time. She called it a "dream vacation."

She met my entire family. She liked them, they liked her. She passed the toughest judgment--Mom gave the big thumbs up. I met her family, I liked them, they liked me. That was so important to her.

We were with each other a portion of nearly every day. We talked about possibly living together and taking trips. Our future looked promising.

But all wasn't perfect in Laguna Beach. We both dragged baggage into the relationship. My 1994 was filled with separation and divorce so I was dealing with the pain and bitterness of that. Also, a summer relationship left mixed emotions still tugging on me.

And yet, I knew the widow was special. She had a lot to offer. I tried to put my heart into "us" as best I could. There were times when I knew I was coming up short. Some things can't be faked.

Her suitcases likewise were heavy. She never properly mourned the lost of a "perfect husband." They knew each other 38 years and were a couple for 18. Six months after he died, she tried to fill his void by getting involved with another man. They dated one year. That relationship added more baggage to ours.

I often heard about the husband and the other gentleman. Made it difficult on me, but then again I talked about my relationships so it sort of made us even.

When she called one Monday night to tell me it was over, I was somewhat relieved. We had been trying to force the relationship. Deep inside I didn't believe it was really over but a vacation from each other was fine with me. It would give us both a chance to recheck our feelings on our recent relationships.

A funny thing started to happen. After a few days, I found myself thinking frequently of her. During the two months, she had grown on me. More than I realized. So, when we decided to get together to talk, I was excited.

I promised myself I'd let her be the speaker. She was, but I put in my two cents' worth. She was confused. Missing me but seeing him. Her son told me privately to "just give her some time."

I didn't react well to her telling me about her dates and her new social life. I left in a huff. Upset, I tossed and turned all night. The next morning I called to explain my position, why I reacted the way I did. I told her I cared. She listened. Without further discussion, she said, "It's too bad it has to end this way."

I was stunned but said: "OK." Country and western vocal group, The Mavericks, have a song called, "Oh What A Crying Shame." They sing about a relationship slipping away. How appropriate.

I hung up and wiped away a couple of tears. Sort of foolish for a 55 year-old dude. I realize that timing is everything in a relationship. Ours missed by just a week. Or so it seems.

Middle aged relationships can be tough, we're all so set in our ways. Bummer. Time to pick myself up, to let the foolish dating games begin again. I'll miss the widow.

## Reader Comments and Tom's Responses

Mary, "Before my first date in 29 years, surgery without anesthesia was more welcome. I had a fear of everything. He walks through the door, and wow, much better than my friend the matchmaker described. All went well, I got through it. We plan to meet again. I'm on cloud nine. Was it supposed to be this easy? There is life after divorce. Response: *Good for you. Middle age dating doesn't have to be disastrous. I just seem to invite trouble.*

Jack, "You cared for that widow, but she just wasn't ready. Watch, you'll go away and she'll want to come back. We tend to want what we can't have." Response: *In that case, I'm leaving tomorrow. Do you really think she'll follow?*

## Column 32

# REACTIONS TO "DUMPED BY..."

Last week, I wrote a column entitled, "Dumped by an older-younger woman." There were more responses on my voice mail than from any previous column--so much in fact, I wanted to share some of them with you.

One anonymous woman said: "Even the title irritates me. She's three years younger than you. She's a young whippersnapper. You're the old fart. Keep things in perspective." Now there's a reader who didn't feel very sorry for me.

Neither did Rene. "You described her as older and a widow. That's rude and disparaging. She didn't ask to become a widow. You owe her an apology." Why? For not thanking her adequately for dumping me ungraciously?

Some sympathized. Joyce, Laguna Niguel, said: "You did OK. You had good days and good times with her. It's called learning, maybe lust. When the real thing comes along, you'll know." I met Joyce months ago. She's studied a lot of self-help books, and has a nice outlook on life. The warmth and depth of her comments pleased and surprised me. I disagree with her reference about lust. There wasn't enough sex for lust to be a factor.

Anne, of Dana Point, shared, "I just joined the clan of the recently divorced. Bummer for me too. People are too hard on new singles." Honestly, Anne, I'm beginning to believe I don't understand women.

# MIDDLE AGED AND DATING AGAIN

From Laguna Hills, Don offered: "I'm 58, my wife died a year ago. I've found a new life country and western dancing. Go to Duke's at the Hyatt Newporter on Friday nights--you'll find good fun. Lots of pretty ladies." Don, I'll meet you there. You'll probably be the one with a woman on each arm. Good for you.

Claudia, Foothill Ranch, threw a little encouragement my way, "From your picture, you are very handsome. You'll have no problem getting a nice woman. Don't force it. If you do, it won't work." I have new glasses so the paper took a new picture. The new picture makes me look worse than the old picture did. Maybe I need to see a plastic surgeon.

Rita, Dana Point, has managed to keep a positive attitude despite being a widow of two years, and now losing her job of 25 years. "Regarding that woman who said you are whimping along, at least you are honest about your feelings. A lot of single people don't admit they're vulnerable, that they hurt. You have guts. You should feel good about yourself and forget about that woman Micholena, she's a witch. By the way, where does your widow friend meet men?"

I'll forget about Micholena, sounds like she's not my type anyway. As for the widow, how does she find men? She traps them in her web. She tracked me down in my deli. Claims she had no intention to date, just to say "hello." Hogwash. I could see that gleam in her eyes when she walked into my deli. She wasn't looking for a roast beef sandwich.

Maybe a woman in Birmingham, Michigan, age 51, has the right idea. She rented a full-size billboard for $2,000 for a month which read, "I'm Tired of Being Single." Her picture is on it. So far, 35 men have responded. Maybe one of them will fill the bill. Or, er, pay the bills.

Isn't being middle aged and single just a blast?

## Readers Comments and Tom's Responses

Rene, "I'm the person who said you should apologize to the widow. My reason is you called her a name in the paper. When you refer to a person as a widow, I picture a black widow spider crawling around in the corner--it's a creepy title for a person.

"Also, you should consider the Divorce Recovery Workshop at Saddleback Community Church. I've been single 44 years and have much insight. When you're out there looking for somebody, that's what you'll find, **some body.** Lots of people are struggling to find a purpose."

Response: *I will continue to call her "the widow" because that's my affectionate name for her. When I picture the widow, I see a very special woman, not a spider. She's been through more adversity recently than most people suffer in a lifetime. As for the workshop you suggest, I didn't get divorced from her, just dumped after a short relationship. I'm trying to find a purpose all right, why did she do it? Furthermore, some "body" is better than no "body," at least in my arms, if only on a temporary basis. Willie Nelson sang a song about one night a week is better than no nights a week, and he wasn't referring to going to church. And you, single for 44 years???*

## Column 33

# BASKETBALL OVER PASTA

I asked a new acquaintance for a date. She threw me a curve. "Love to, but that night is my son's last basketball game before the playoffs begin. May we do that first?"

St. Margaret's vs. Capo Valley Christian, Tartans vs. Eagles. A couple of San Juan Capistrano private high schools with a cross town rivalry as hot as M.I.T.-Harvard.

It's important, of course, for mom to be there before tip off. A 7:30 p.m. start will put us in front of a plate of pasta by 9:30 p.m. We arrive on time. My stomach groans when we discover the girls' game beforehand is just starting the third quarter, 45 minutes behind schedule.

To hold us, we settle for a couple of pieces of booster club pizza. They're cold. She says she likes it that way. I remind myself that I'm not at Prego or some other fancy Italian restaurant, and should be grateful just for something to eat.

It's been a long time since I attended a basketball game where there's no charge for admission. We enter the little gym. She's uncomfortable. It seems the eyes of the world are checking us out. I whisper, "People seem to be noticing you're with somebody new." Straightfaced, she counters, "People are noticing I'm with *somebody period.*"

My date was married to a successful basketball coach. She knows the game well. Early on, she tells me, "Two things which bug me are no defense and poor offensive rebounding." Late in the third quarter she yells at her son, "You're forcing your shot. Meet the ball. Stop dogging it, you can rest later." If the Tartans' coach is ever ejected, it's obvious whom they'll get from the bleachers to fill in.

Her son commits his second foul. A woman friend sitting next to her says, "You didn't bring him up right."

Least interested fan is Chelsea, a 3 year-old beauty wearing a red Tartans T-shirt over her Sunday dress. Chelsea arrives with an armful of dolls which are spread out around her. She offers me a teddy bear to hold. For most of the game she tends to her mother's hair, with a comb and some melted chocolate chips. When someone yells, "Fire up Tartans," Chelsea asks why they are being fired. Her mom tries to explain firing up and being fired are different.

My date's son cans a couple of late free throws. "Good ball rotation," she shouts. He drives the length of the court, makes a cross over dribble, and hits an off-balance jump shot. A proud parent smiles.

The Tartans win, advancing to the C.I.F. playoffs. It's like Hoosier mania right here in the heart of Capo Valley.

Finally, at 11:00 p.m., we are served pasta at a restaurant in town. Over dinner, she confesses it's her first date in 27 years with anyone besides her ex-husband.

## Reader Comments and Tom's Responses

Lori, "You made it sound like giving up your pasta dinner until 11:00 p.m. was a big sacrifice for you." Response: *It was. I'm usually in bed by eleven.*

Beth: "That basketball date knows more about the game than you do about the games you seem to play." Response: *Wait a minute, she was married to a coach for over 20 years. I've only been dating for a year.*

Larry: "Can she dunk?" Response: *What? A ball?*

## Column 34

# BEWARE WHEN YOU HEAR, "I NEED SPACE"

You're cruising along in your new middle age relationship. It was hard to find somebody compatible. At first, both were cautious. Slowly, you begin to trust. You like her. She likes you. There are some minor bumps to sandpaper but you're adults. Mature, able to talk about differences, to meet halfway. You're tolerant, and accepting each other's baggage .

After a month, your words just slip out: "I *could* love you *someday."* Not an unconditional, "I love you," but a start. A week later, in aisle 4 at Hughes Market, she says "I love you." You take her hand, look in her eyes, and think middle-aged relationships can be special. Slowly, yours is growing, and it feels good.

You put forth more energy than you did in any of your three marriages. You serve her coffee in bed, pick up her cat at the vet, and clean up after the dog. But then, it's your dog who is messing up her yard. She likes being nurtured. You're helping each other. You start to believe you might end up together. Friends say you're both lucky, family members are buzzing.

Out of the blue one night, she hands you a card: "This is going to surprise you. There's an incredible bond--we've become very close. I am becoming a bit scared. I'm feeling the need to withdraw a little, **not breakup**--not stay apart, but just give each other a little *space."*

# MIDDLE AGED AND DATING AGAIN

"SPACE" The "S" word. The red flag for relationships worldwide. It means all's not well in river city. Like the board game from Toys 'R Us, applicable to ages 6-66. When you hear the words, take heed.

"Gee, what brought this on?" you ask. She answers: "I can't give you all you want."

You've never asked for much. "All I want is your old boyfriend to stop calling at midnight, and for you not to sneak in the living room and talk to him for 20 minutes while I'm pretending to be sleeping. Is that an unreasonable request after being together for five months?" She thinks it is.

You're middle aged, you thought the games were behind you. You didn't expect the frigid turn of events. You go searching for space. Because it's invisible, you go far into the universe.

You foolishly return time and time again, because she wants to see you and you're too weak to say no. And you love her. Finally, one time you don't return, you realize it's futile. You discover there are others out there who want and will appreciate what you can offer.

You're reminded of the message from a 1970s Jackson Browne song, *Fountain of Sorrow*. People look for perfect love, and when they don't find it, they go looking for it. They never find it so loneliness springs from their life "like a fountain from a pool." She's a fountain. You're a fountain. Both lonely fountains.

Your faith in middle aged relationships is shaken. She's got her space. Your dog is back home. And you're out there looking again, free falling through space.

## Reader Comments and Tom's Responses

Frank: "Your articles are great. You are talented. I love your satirical twists and humor. Too bad the paper won't give you a little more space." Response: *The paper gave me more "space" this week. The entire column was devoted to the word. Unfortunately, the woman also gave me some "space."*

Eddie: "Regarding space, I had the same experience with a woman. Maybe they are going through a stage in life--flakey and difficult. I've had friends experience the same thing. That's why I don't date." Response: *Why don't we start a "space" camp, where, when you hear the word, you put on your space helmet, and then go looking for a spacey woman.*

Patti: "If you serve her coffee in bed, she should be talking commitment, instead of space." Response: *That's the way I felt about it.*

Connie: "Where does middle age end and senior age begin?" Response: *In one's head. Age is just a state of mind, it's up to you. This isn't like being old enough to vote, or drink, or drive.*

## Column 35

# DON'T DRINK DOWNSTREAM FROM THE HORSES

Middle aged, dating, and wondering what to do? Take a ride to Julian, "The queen of the back country." It's a gold mining town 60 miles east of Oceanside. About a two hour drive from South Orange County.

A woman invited me to join three generations of her family for a visit. Grandma, 31 year-old son and wife, 16 year-old son, and 3 year-old granddaughter, piled in a Jeep Cherokee. I'm grandma's date.

Before leaving the city limits of Dana Point, eight Snapples and four bags of chips are consumed. "Where's the Kleenex?" and. "Are we there yet?" are asked.

Middle aged daters should be willing to try new things. I painfully remind myself we aren't driving to South Bend, or Ann Arbor, for a football game. After all, it's a Saturday in the fall. Six of us in the Jeep means one has to sit cross ways in the rear, with one's feet stuck in the spare tire, legs and vertebrae bent uncomfortably. Despite being the oldest, I do my turn back there, wondering if I'm being tested, hoping she'll appreciate my sacrifice of an aching back.

Curvy highway 76 takes us through the Pala Indian Reservation. We arrive at lunchtime. BBQ beef, pork ribs, and chicken are specials we order at the historic Bailey Barbecue. The restaurant's address hints at the size of the town--the intersection of Main and A streets.

Just above the restaurant is the Pioneer Cemetery which reminds me of Boot Hill. At work, a lonely gravedigger--it sort of gives me the willie's. Makes you wonder who's headed up there. Glad I ate before seeing that scene.

In and out of shops. In and out of shops. My head is spinning. She asks, "This isn't your bag, is it?" I smile, wondering if the Michigan football team has scored yet, but knowing dessert is just around the corner.

At 4500 feet, apples grow abundantly in the clean air on the green hillsides. The smell of hot apple cider permeates the town. The big attraction is the hot apple pie. We take ours at The Julian Pie Company, a quaint place with a swing out back. After the best pie topped with the best cinnamon ice cream I've ever had, the granddaughter joins me on the swing. She wants to go higher and higher. I'm petrified she'll fall off. Don't want to be responsible for that. This isn't a fifty yard-line seat. Then, again, maybe it is.

Tourists everywhere carry boxes of pies. The Julian Cider Mill advertises honey bees for sale.

Three horse-drawn carriages for hire soften the town. Bed and breakfast inns and lodges abound. The cutest name in a town full of cute names--The Wikiup B & B.

Signs outside the Julian Country Store read, "Always drink upstream from the herd," and "Buggy parking only." They remind me we aren't at glitzy Fashion Island in Newport Beach.

At the Julian Town Hall craft show, I purchase a refrigerator door magnet--a wooden red apple with "Julian, Ca." painted on it. Hoping she'll remember I was along, it's left on her Kenmore refrigerator door.

A long roundtrip--over four hours in the car--but worth it. A California gem near our back yard.

## Reader Comments and Tom's Responses

Jan: "I'm happily married. If I were looking for a man, I'd want one willing to sit crunched up in the back of a car and willing to push a 3-year old on a swing." Response: *Someone noticed, thank you. Oh, my aching back.*

Carol: "It seems you and this woman, if it's the same one, do lots together and yet she is confused." Response: *If you think she's confused, you can imagine how I feel.*

Betsy: "I could taste the apple pie." Response: *So could I, all the way home.*

# MIDDLE AGED AND DATING AGAIN

## COLUMN 36

# THE $38 MOTEL ROOM

Along with 600 others, I attended a writer's conference at San Diego State University recently. Some attendees were successful authors, others were hoping to be. Writers are dedicated. For this conference, they gave up their Saturdays and Sundays. Most shelled out nearly $300 from their own pockets to improve their skills.

About 70% who went were women. Pretty good odds for a middle aged and dating gentleman who might be looking for a date. But I've learned from previous conferences one doesn't go to find a date. Most are geographically undesirable, living in places such as San Diego, Carlsbad, La Jolla, or Phoenix. No one else had "Dana Point" on their name tag. Besides, my mom says I don't always need a date when I go somewhere. I agree. I was there professionally.

For most women writers, dating is not their top priority. Manicures and pedicures are of lesser importance than a good session in front of their word processors.

My purpose in going was to find a literary agent to help me publish a middle age dating guidebook. Agents are treated like the Hope diamond because most writers feel to get published a good agent is needed.

At the conference, agents were pestered all of the time. During meals, people stopped to ask them questions, even if one had just taken a bite of lasagna. A patient but exasperated agent was off in a corner preparing two writing critiques, due in 10 minutes. During that short span, she was interrupted five times (once by me). She told me to mail her a book proposal. In ten seconds, my goal for the week-end had been accomplished.

Confession: I didn't go date-free. A friend hopped Amtrak in San Juan Capistrano late Saturday afternoon to join me. Our motel was the Good Nite Inn. Not because I'm cheap. The conference promoters had struck a deal there and it was close to the campus. Only double beds were available. Bummer. Sort of uncool telling your lady you're switching hotels because you want a king size bed. For $38, what did I expect? Besides, the room was prepaid.

She had no comment about the three dead bolts on the door, the missing door knobs, and the extra thick chain and double lock on the sliding glass door. Even the television channel changer was secured to the nightstand. About 1 a.m., we heard screams coming from inside the motel.

She was a good sport, murmuring, "The room is clean; the front desk people are nice." At some ungodly hour, she called her 16 year-old to be sure he had gotten home before his curfew.

On Sunday morning, we found a Danish restaurant called Dansk in La Mesa Village. Eggs Florentine on a Belgian waffle and Swedish pancakes got the nod. She suggested we try dinner there some night. I agreed, but felt driving 75 miles a bit far. Of course, we could stay at the Good Nite Inn again. Was the week-end worth the bucks? Yes, if a book gets published.

## Reader Comments and Tom's Responses

Gayle: "I can't believe you had a date come down and stay in such a dive. She rode the train and went to all that trouble to stay in a dump. Were there any rats in the room besides you? You're cheap." Response: *The room had nice towels.*

Betsy: "If you took me to a $38 motel, I'd never see you again." Response: *She isn't, but not for that reason.*

Patty: "Regarding that woman who was critical of the $38 motel room: What's the difference, if a room's $38 or $500? It's not the price of the room but the quality of the person you're with. People around here put too much emphasis on the value of the dollar. At least you didn't make her curl up in a sleeping bag." Response: *I keep one rolled up in the back of my car for such emergencies.*

Deborah: "I know you are wondering where all the single women to date are in Orange County. We read your articles, but no, we don't want to date you." *Thank God, there are a few left who do.*

Carolyn: "I took your advice and broke up with the married guy. Maybe we're all looking too hard--sometimes we push it. We hope this one works and then that one. When we're older, it's harder to find someone. Blending families, interests, things like that--a lot of complicated issues." *Yup, some of us are looking too hard. Might I be one of them?*

## COLUMN 37

# A DATE WITH MY HIGH SCHOOL SWEETHEART

The phone call came: "Hi, Tom, it's Mary Mac. I'll be in Southern California soon. May I visit you?" The voice: My high school sweetheart of 40 years ago. Class of '57. Jackson High. Jackson, Michigan. Mary's pending visit upset the woman I'm dating.

Under Mary's yearbook picture: "Most likely to succeed." Under mine: "Most sincere." Was Mary like George Foreman, looking for a rematch? Mary wasn't my first love, my heart had been broken by Patty Toms in the eighth grade.

In 1955, while sitting across from each other in study hall, Mary invited me to a Xmas dance. On January 9, 1956, we agreed to go steady.

Once, she told me we should date others. That hurt but I quickly countered by taking Sandy Buxton to the drive-in. The next morning Mary asked me to pick her up from church. I did. She cried. From then until graduation, we were the "perfect couple."

That summer, she went to Europe. I missed her. I shook from excitement when she stepped off the plane at Willow Run Airport in Detroit. The big hurt started that night, she didn't want to be boyfriend-girlfriend anymore.

# MIDDLE AGED AND DATING AGAIN

The ache lasted 4 years. I learned how to play it cool, to construct walls around myself, and cut my vulnerability. I got street-wise dating.

She married a lawyer from the Michigan Law School. I embarked on a career of chasing women. They had four kids. After her last child left for college, they divorced, realizing they'd stayed together just for the children. She moved to Washington, D.C., finding life in a new city, especially *that* one, difficult for a middle aged single woman. Now she's got this thing about reconnecting with old pals.

I married and divorced three times. No kids. Never willing to stay in relationships that weren't right.

Mary arrived. We drove around Dana Point in a driving rain. There was no dinner out. In my kitchen, she warmed some left over soup she'd gotten from my deli, cut up a pear, and had some carrot and celery sticks. The whole scenario reminded me of that song about the couple who ran into each other Christmas Eve, and drank a six-pack in the car, while talking of old times.

While reminiscing, I remembered an old scrap book I had with some newspaper clippings about her dad's death in 1965, and my dad's death in 1966. Her dad did a lot for me, and meant a lot to me. The dusty book was found in a weathered box in the garage. It was dedicated to her dad, JFK, and the 129 men of the USS Thresher, a nuclear submarine that had disintegrated underwater. She was overwhelmed. As we looked over the material, our eyes watered. It was a warm moment. I promised I'd make copies to send her.

At 7 p.m, she left for LAX to catch a flight to Cincinnati. No hanky-panky, or old fires rekindled. Nothing for my present lady to worry about. I haven't heard from Mary since.

As we age, connecting with old friends becomes important to us. Our current loves need to understand, as we do about them connecting with their old friends. It's no threat to existing relationships, just something we must do.

## Reader Comments and Tom's Responses

Fran: "Sounds like you didn't treat your former love very well." Response: *Yea, guess I should have at least taken her to dinner. I was trying not to upset my current lady friend.*

Lorraine: "Was it strange seeing a girlfriend of 40 years ago?" Response: *It was like, where did the 40 years go?*

Cathy: "Maybe check her out at the next class reunion." Response: *Jackson, Michigan, is a long way to travel from California.*

## COLUMN 38

# WHO PAYS FOR THE DATE?

You're a hard working, enlightened, and proud woman of the 90s, at a restaurant with a date. The bill arrives. You whip out your Visa card, handing it to the waiter. Your date is dumbfounded, about to object. You're beaming, and you say, "My treat."

The server returns the little brown tray with your credit card voucher to be signed. And places it *in front of your date*. What an insult--a clueless server. It's happened before, it will happen again. Some people don't understand it's OK for women to pay for dates. When a woman pays, men should accept the gesture graciously. They should appreciate that their date wants to share in the cost of dating. If men are so macho or unenlightened they won't let women pay, they deserve to have their pockets emptied.

I met a women for a breakfast blind date at IHOP. She insisted on going dutch. A reader commented, "You're cheap, you wouldn't pay for Jean's breakfast." My response: *"Jean insisted, she wanted no obligation. In fact, she couldn't get away from me fast enough."*

A safe rule of thumb: the person who initiates the date, who asks the other out, should pay. If a woman seeks the pleasure of a man's company, it's on her nickel. And vice versa. In the 90s, it's acceptable for women to ask men out.

The other night, a woman asked me to meet her for a glass of wine. When the bill came, she bailed to the restroom. I'll never go out with her again, not because she didn't pay, but because I didn't enjoy her company. Still, she should have paid.

If two people develop a relationship, they need to reach an understanding on finances. If he takes her to dinner, she can reciprocate by having him over for dinner.

A man wants to take his woman to Mexico for three days, his treat, to show her she's special. If she's wise, she'll buy the margaritas on the beach or spring for dinner one night.

The "who pays?" issue isn't simply a question of who can afford it the most. It's both contributing to the relationship. If he's broke and she's wealthy, and she always pays, he'd better contribute to the relationship in other ways.

I dated a woman for a few months. I always paid because she was struggling financially. She said, "I know you've been spending a lot of money on me lately, but I'd like to see the ballet." I knew she was inheriting a substantial amount of money soon so I replied, "Why don't we go dutch?" She went ballistic. "I've never, ever, ever paid a penny on a date!" Oh boy, a relationship danger signal. She expected the man to always pay. The funny thing was, she didn't have much to offer in other ways. Shortly thereafter, we stopped dating.

A bit of advice. If you're invited to your date's church, drop some bucks in the collection plate, whether your date does or not.

## Reader Comments and Tom's Responses

Carolyn: "If you want to date us, you've got to pay. The meaner I am, the more men like me." *Carolyn, Carolyn, I'm surprised at you. You're usually so enlightened. Did we get you on a bad day? If spending $45 for a hour and a half date is your idea of fun and fairness, you won't get many second offers. Maybe the reason there are so many men lined up at your door is because you're mean, but that won't work for long either.*

Marie: "I wouldn't mind paying my share if I only could find a guy I like." Response: *Dating at middle age is a numbers game. Keep active and get out of the house. You'll find someone.*

Jane: "That woman who went ballistic about the ballet, get rid of her. She's carrying too much baggage." Response: *Yea, she thinks men owe her just for the pleasure of her company. What a joke.*

## Column 39

# DATING WITH KIDS STILL AROUND

One of the challenging issues for single middle agers can be dating someone with children still living at home. When people date and no children are around, each can focus on the relationship. No baby sitters needed. You can smooch and not worry about little Johnny tying your shoelaces together.

Mix in a few kids, the puzzle becomes more complex. I never had children. Most women I've dated do, many with children living at home. The scenarios are endless.

I meet a woman with 13 and 17 year olds living with her. The relationship grows. Both would like to spend some intimate time together. You're a couple of caged cats. You ask, "When will we be able to spend the night together?" She replies, "On every other Saturday, when the children go to their father's." Then the father cancels. Willie Nelson sang something about one night of loving is better than no nights of loving. Suppose Willie's right, but two weeks seems like a long time between nights. You're not in prison. In a way you are.

You could sneak a "quickie" when the kids aren't looking. At our age, we have to do that? Seems cheap, hurried, tacky, and unfulfilling.

One woman recently told me her 11 year-old daughter gave her permission to go out with me. Next time, I'll probably get permission directly from the daughter.

A buddy of mine was invited to a woman's house on valentine's day. She greeted him wearing a sultry red outfit. The woman taped a note in the shape of a heart on the front door: "Valentines at play, do not disturb."

"Why the sign?" my friend asked. "In case my daughter, Missy, comes home. She usually just barges in. This way, let's hope she'll knock first." My friend couldn't relax. Valentines didn't play.

The combination of--one party having children and the other not-- can work well. I was in a pretty ideal situation. With no children, I could always be with hers on holidays. An added bonus--I liked them, they liked me. I enjoyed watching sports events on television with her boys. Last XMAS, I spent the day with my mom in Santa Rosa and the night with her family in Irvine.

When both dating parties have children, the waters get a little muddier. It's Thanksgiving. You and your sweetie want to be together. She wants to be with her kids, you with yours. You try to merge the families. But you're not big on hers and she's not big on yours. Yours don't like her and they can't stand hers. Hers don't like you and they can't stand yours. Sounds like a card table scene from the movie, *The Outcasts of Poker Flats*.

Children must be the top priority. Most everyone agrees. Whether a couple can function happily under that umbrella depends on how important the relationship is to each. If both are mature and patient, somehow, it'll work out.

"Pass the turkey, bozo."
"What for, you jerk!"
"Children, children, please!"

## Reader Comments and Tom's Responses

Woman in hair salon:  "Here comes the man who is so big on children."  Response: *I do love children.  I said they must be the top priority, but I like a hug once in a while also.*

Christine: "Why didn't you have children?  It's probably because you couldn't hold a wife long enough to conceive.  Response: *Now, is that nice?  I just couldn't afford to send them to college.*

Carolyn:  "Children must be the top priority and we must set an example for our kids.  I suggest having your child or children go stay at a friend's house if you want to be alone with a man.  Then, return the favor for a friend.  Be discreet but have some fun."  Response: *I made a deal with a woman friend's child.  I agreed to mow the lawn for him if he'd stay at his cousin Billy's house on a Saturday night.  He said "no" unless I also paid him $5. Everybody won but I was out five bucks.*

## Column 40

# HIGH EXPECTATIONS AND
# A DANCEBAND

Where can 163 of the classiest, most eligible, middle-aged singles be found in South Orange County? At our second middle-aged singles gathering, which took place at the Dana Point Resort on Friday, March 3rd.

Penny, recently of Scottsdale, Arizona, was one of the first to arrive. She said: "The last party I went to had 32 women and one man. I hope tonight won't be like that. " At that time, the only other people present were, Dennis, of Dana Point; Geri, our hard working, efficient, hostess; and me. Looking at the two attractive women, Dennis responded, "Let's close down now and go have our own private party." Dennis has always been a hound.

The ratio this time was better, still not 50% men but closer. Regardless, all seemed to enjoy themselves. Jennifer, from San Juan Capistrano, had her miniature dog inside her coat, probably to keep the wolves away.

I overheard Roberta, also of San Juan Capistrano, say, "I've got six Chinese Shar-Peis and not one of them can dial 911." What's the deal with dogs in San Juan?

The comments ranged from, "I enjoy your columns," to, "Where's the widow?" to, "You look younger than your picture." One woman from Rancho Santa Margarita said our crowd wasn't the "needy" type she sees at organized singles functions.

Jo, Mission Viejo, who works for this newspaper, said we were more organized than the newsroom. Ed Conway, a columnist, also for this paper, was seen soliciting. Probably material for his column.

Bill, Mission Viejo, the reader who told me to dye my hair, kept pointing to his, saying, "See, see, see--look what a difference darker makes." He didn't exactly have a harem hanging off of his arm.

At one point, somebody's drink trickled down my pantleg, off my sock, and into my shoe. Must have been a drink--it was cold.

Bob, who looks 10 years younger than I, but is 10 years older, said he's never been married. I've been married three times. Is there a message?

Candy, San Juan Capistrano, attended, bless her heart. She has four kids and a missing-in-action husband. Despite a tough road, she found the strength to show up. I even received a grammar lesson, of course. When to use who vs. whom. A woman said to substitute he for who and him for whom, it'll work everytime.

Sue, from Adrian, Mich., looked smashing in a white dress. The party started at 7 p.m. A combo played until 8:45. The dance band started in the bar at 9. A woman came up to me at 9:10 and asked, "Now what happens?" I didn't know how to respond, but told her there was a snipe hunt starting on the hotel grounds.

Will romances bloom? Don't know. Some phone numbers changed hands. As for me, I slipped out the side door at 10:30 p.m., unable to choose from all of the fine women present.

# Reader comments and Tom's Responses

Anonymous Woman: "At the next singles function, we need more men." Response: *I agree. We tried. Next time, we'll invite the Navy.*

Carolyn: "Next time, have all the women bring their old boyfriends." Response: *And what? Dump them off on someone else?*

Jack: "I had a terrific time. Some people didn't because in my opinion, their expectations are too high. Why not go and just have a good time, even if you don't meet a new dating partner? Response: *Well stated. People at our age often have their expectations too high.*

## COLUMN 41

# BY NOW, I SHOULD HAVE LEARNED

This wasn't a blind date but a first date. My doing. I asked her out. She spotted me running my dog on the beach near the Ritz Carlton Hotel. She stared and smiled. A pretty brunet, friendly, about 37 years old.

"You write that singles column, don't you? The one on *space* hit home, it had meaning for me." We walk up the hill to the Salt Creek Beach parking lot. She wants to get together. I should have wondered then and there what she saw in a guy almost 20 years older. But all I could think of was taking out this pretty lady.

"I have a 13 year-old daughter living at home so during the week I don't date because I'm with her. When she goes to her father's on certain week-ends, I can go out. But I could meet you for walks in the morning." Her comments are relationship incompatibility warning signs. I ignore them. I think of her green eyes and flashing smile. Later, a Saturday night date is made. She said her daughter gave approval. That's scary.

More warning signs surface: "Call before picking me up, I'll meet you in the auto turn-around circle." I wonder why she doesn't want me to come to her front door?

In my car, she tells me she doesn't want to go far away for dinner. I think that's a pretty strange request. I didn't exactly have Las Vegas in mind. She insists on the geographically *closest* restaurant, about a mile away. She explains her daughter is home alone and mama wants to remain nearby.

I've heard the suggested restaurant is expensive. Dropping a big wad on a shaky first date isn't smart. But, I agree because neither of us have been there before.

At the restaurant, she calls to check on her daughter. I whisper: "Give her the restaurant telephone number." She covers the phone mouthpiece, "I can handle this on my own." I've insulted her by trying to be nice. We're already at odds. We haven't been seated yet.

Somehow, we have a nice dinner. I plop down $45, not as much as anticipated. It's early--9 p.m. We've been out only a little over an hour. Knowing she's concerned about her daughter, I make a suggestion, "Let's grab a bottle of wine. We can share a glass at your place and be with your daughter."

"I want no men in my home while my 11 year-old daughter's there." Earlier, she mentioned her daughter was 13. Why the discrepancy? Did her daughter shrink in age while we were over pasta in the last hour?

"You mean, if we date, I can't come to your house if your daughter's there?" "Not for 6 months." A chill envelops a warm restaurant. In the car she asks, "Where are you going now?"

"I am taking you home, but if you'd rather go somewhere else, we can. I just didn't want to sit in an Italian restaurant drinking $7 glasses of wine."

"Take me home." I ask, "Why didn't you want me to come to your door?" "Laura Schlesinger on KFI radio said it's cool, makes men guess." Near her apartment, she says, "Let's talk tomorrow." I walk away, scratching my head, thinking she must be joking.

I've been dating 16 months. You'd think by now I'd have learned to prequalify my dates.

## Reader Comments and Tom's Responses

Phil: "You was used." Response: *I guess I need to be more patient or something. She was pretty protective of her daughter. I think she's looking for a buddy type of arrangement. Still, spending money for a short date wasn't worth it.*

Doris: "If you're dumb enough to take her out, you deserve what you got." Response: *Doris dear, that attitude is what puts men and women at odds.*

Jake: "You paid the price for dating a beautiful women." Response: *It's that simple?*

Vicki: "No woman wants you in her place on the first date. You just want to spend the least amount of money to get what you can. I'm kind of losing respect for you." Response: *Is that why women never want to come to my place on the first date?*

## COLUMN 42

# DATING ALEXANDER HAIG

You're middle aged. You lose your loved one through death or divorce. Maybe you knew it was coming, maybe you didn't. Regardless, now you're the person Paul Simon sings about in "Graceland." You've lost your love, you're devastated, blown apart, and everybody knows it.

You're debilitated, can't function, you feel like engineer Casey Jones in the *Wreck of the Old 97*. Sunrises and sunsets don't matter to you. And life doesn't much either.

You force yourself to attend grief counseling or a divorce recovery workshop. They tell you, "The only way to heal is from within first. Learn to like yourself. Learn to be an individual again." The long road back begins. One hour at a time. You have setbacks along the way.

You hear, "You can't advance time and time is what it takes." You're weak, vulnerable, and lonely. Along comes Mr. Fix-it. A buddy, at first, someone to lean on. You talk, he listens. He's there for you. He gives you advice, he mows your yard. He holds your hand and drys your tears. You appreciate him although you grieve.

You're beginning to rely on him because it's easy. He senses you need him. He starts to see you as more than just a buddy. He loves you. It becomes his mission to help you through widowdum or divorcedum.

He starts making decisions for you. He organizes your cupboards and orders your child around. The kid resents it. He tells you how to recover. He asks you not to talk about your ex anymore because now he's the man in your life.

Who's in control here?

- Not you, you're just trying to get by.
- Not Alexander Haig, he never was, he just thought he was.
- Mr. Fix-it is. And every day he wants to control you more. Mr. Fix-it believes he's Alexander Haig.

You're living a second tragedy, you're allowing it to happen. He's a good person but you know you will never love him. Now, you're afraid you'll hurt him.

You're in a bind--being controlled, but grateful for the early assistance. You've always had a strong male in your life to help make your decisions, a father figure. He's become one. And you're a whimp.

You're like a country receiving foreign aid as directed by the Secretary of State. You accept it, but resent it. You need to break away. Time has helped you heal but you're stuck in remote control, because he's got the clicker. And you haven't really healed because he's been in the way when you needed time to yourself.

You feel guilty because you want him to release you. He says: "Look at all I've done for you. You're my everything, my whole life." You keep reminding yourself he's not a bad person. His granddaughters call: "We love you Auntie Mame. Be nice to our grandpa." You die because you love these children. For the time in two years, you're being ripped apart. Once from a death, now from a life.

Twice you've made the break. You even dated another man you think you love. The other man sees you're controlled by Alexander. He's been patient. How much longer will he be? How much longer can he be? Does losing him matter to you?

It's time to step to the plate. You need to be in control here. You are so unsettled.

## Reader Comments and Tom's Responses

Alexander: "My name is Alexander Haig. No, I'm not the famous one. Stop saying you're dating me and never trust a woman who listens to Laura Schlesinger on KFI. You won't find me at the Nixon compound this week-end. I love you. I salute you and God bless America." Response: *As you can see, this week's column is about women who date men who want to control them, not about me dating Al Haig. I've got my hands full dating her, she still clings to him.*

Anonymous woman: "You're like Alexander Haig, you want to be in control. That was the problem in your three marriages and that's the problem with the woman you wrote about." Response: *Wrong. I've never wanted to control any woman. Relationships need to be balanced 50-50. Sharing and being close are the keys to successful relationships.*

Diane: "That woman needs to get a life." Response: *Slowly, over time, it will work out for her. But yes, she needs to act.*

## COLUMN 43

# WHAT TOM WANTS FROM A RELATIONSHIP

After 17 months of middle aged dating, here's what I want from a relationship:

1. I MUST BE A *TOP PRIORITY* IN HER LIFE.

That's why dating women with children still at home is difficult. The kids need to be her top priority. It takes a rare and caring person who can juggle a man and the kids. We all deserve to be number one in our sweetheart's eyes. We're not chopped liver, although sometimes it feels like it.

2. I WILL NOT *COMPETE* WITH ANOTHER PERSON FOR HER.

I did it for a few days in December and for two months in 1995. I will never do it again. It rips you apart.

3. I WANT A *POSITIVE* INFLUENCE IN MY LIFE.

She's got to be good for me. No negative stuff such as being selfish, or feelings like, "Oh poor me, my life is so tough." I've had enough negative junk over the last 2 years with a divorce, a combative relationship, and a stressful one. We all deserve to be happy.

## 4. NO *EXCESS BAGGAGE.*

We all have some baggage, it goes with the trip. It's the excess to avoid. If she's mired in debt, often depressed, cries for her mother's sympathy, or always talks about her former love, that's excess baggage . There's a host of other things which could come up. Airlines charge premiums for excess baggage--so should we. Carrying our own load is heavy enough.

## 5. IF THE RELATIONSHIP IS *TOO MUCH WORK,* MOVE ON.

Isn't life tough enough these days? If we have to try too hard, it isn't right. A deli customer, Marcia, San Clemente, overheard a buddy's conversation about a difficult relationship. She looked up from her sandwich and said, "If the relationship's always broke, don't try to fix it." Marcia's right. We should have fun because we might not be around tomorrow.

If a relationship isn't working, and we've given it our best shot time after time, it's probably taking a physical toll on us. We're stressed. We might not be getting enough sleep. Maybe we start smoking again or drinking too much. *GET OUT! IT'S NOT HEALTHY.*

## 6. A RELATIONSHIP MUST HAVE *CHEMISTRY, ATTRACTION, and AFFECTION.*

A little intimacy helps. A lot helps more. The spark's got to be there or forget all of this other stuff.

7. *COMMUNICATION* MUST BE WORKING.  BOTH MUST WANT TO TRY.

We must be able to talk to each other, to listen, hear, and understand our mate.  Relationships don't thrive on guesswork.  If communication's not happening, move on, it won't work.  Talk without screaming at your mate.

****

As we grow older, we become more and more set in our ways. To find a partner who satisfies most of the above conditions is a big task.  No wonder it's so hard to find somebody compatible.

## Reader Comments and Tom's Responses

Diane:  "Good column, but are you really living it?"  Response: *Bang.  Tom's been shot and hit by Diane.  I'm doing my best. I said, that's what I want in a relationship, not necessarily, what I'm getting.*

Sue:  "Add to your list:  Couples need to enjoy being with each other's friends.  Also, from a woman's viewpoint, does the man respect his mother?"  Response: *Good points.  The list could be lengthened.  That's how I felt at the moment.*

Lana:  "What do you mean by 'top priority?' "  Response: *I want to be more important to her than Grannie Grunts and Uncle Bixby.*

## COLUMN 44

# BUT SHE WAS BEAUTIFUL

An attractive brunet stopped by my deli to ask a question about becoming an entrepreneur. Subsequently, we met twice for drinks at night.

After a 32-year abusive marriage, she was still involved in an unhappy 3-year relationship which she said was nearing an end. She was enthusiastic: "It's time for me to date new people." She had twin 34 year-old daughters. From the information she revealed, I estimated her to be 53, if she married at age 16. She looked 40. There wasn't a wrinkle on her face. She could pass for Sophia Lauren, body and all. She was beautiful.

We agreed to go out on a Saturday night. She wanted it to be special. I let her book the reservation. Prego, in Irvine, was her choice, not exactly the cheapest restaurant in Orange County.

At her front door, I handed her a rose, cut 10 minutes before from my patio. She looked beautiful in a daring black outfit, the yellow rose attached. I hoped we'd run into *anybody* who knew me.

The waiter suggested a $25 bottle of Silverado Chardonnay--I winced, but wanted this night to be the start of many more with her. We talked about her. I asked all of the questions. She relished the attention. "What's so special about this guy you've been dating?" was the first thing I wanted to know.

"He treats me like hell, but we have an incredible sex life." Now there was a comment to get the old imagination flowing. I shuddered, picturing the scene. I wondered how anyone could mistreat this Italian beauty? Visions of romantic moments with her got my heart started.

I said: "After so many difficult years, you deserve a really nice guy in your life." I wanted to add, "like me," but didn't. She never asked about me. But she was beautiful.

Toward the end of dinner, out of the blue, she said, "AIDS changes things--I won't be intimate with another man until I've known him 6 months." Why did she say that? Was she testing me? Six months seems like such a long time.

For the second Saturday night in a row, a chill set in over my table at a fine Orange County Italian restaurant. Her comment was directed at me. Or maybe, just men in general.

I started to debate: "There are ways to protect..." but stopped. Why even bother? If that's the way she feels, I'm not going to make it my project to change her thinking.

She wasn't done: "The most important thing to you is a commitment, a relationship. I don't want that." Where did she get that? She'd been the center of attention all night. The only questions I'd answered were the waiter's. Had I been too aggressive by opening her car door? I hadn't even held her hand. Conversation crumbled. My seat cushion turned to stone. The music died. The waiter was summoned. The $88 tab paid.

Has a drive from Irvine to Dana Point ever been so silent? Why had the night turned sour? Two and a half hours after walking down her front steps together, I watched her walk up alone. She never turned around. She had nice legs.

I felt foolish, used, and empty. She needed to be dominated. I was too nice to her. We haven't spoken since. But she was beautiful.

## Reader Comments and Tom's Responses

Julie: "Sounds like you're starting to be a loser-man after 35 years of bad relationships." Response: *And you didn't have the nerve to leave me your phone number.*

Mark: "Never let an unknown woman make the dinner reservations." Response: *You're right. Had I made them, I probably would have saved $40 and had a much shorter drive.*

Bill: "She would have been a tough one to have had a relationship with, too good looking, goes to their head." Response: *But it would have been oh so fun trying.*

Carla: "Thoroughly enjoy your columns. Good to get a man's perspective on things." Response: *Yea, "Men are from Mars...," that's for sure.*

## COLUMN 45

# OFF TO LAS VEGAS WITH THE BOYS

I needed a break from middle aged dating. A bunch of my deli buddies and I left in a rented van for Las Vegas at 1 p.m. on a Friday. Fifteen minutes later, the van stopped at Alicia Parkway to load liquid provisions. Rum and cokes were served before we hit the 405/5 split. The driver didn't drink.

On highway 15 at Norco, a conversation was started at 65mph with three young woman occupying a car in the fast lane who were also on their way to Las Vegas. We invited them to our hotel suite. I guess it's never too soon to start.

At Baker, Calif., which is famous for the tallest thermometer in the world, we had a $1-per-head contest to guess the temperature: 59 degrees.

Took us 9 hours to get to Las Vegas. We stopped at Buffalo Bill's casino at Stateline to leave a few bucks on their tables.

As we came over the final hill where the lights of the city come into view, Tommy T. put a *Viva Las Vegas* Elvis tape into the cassette player. There were hi-fives all around.

Soon, the silliness began. Thirteen guys in a 2-bedroom $500 per night penthouse suite at Bally's. Beds for about six to sleep. No way, I'm too old for that. Bruce and I got our own room at the Comfort Inn.

Friday night found us at the Horseshoe Casino with the rest of the cheap-o's who part with their money downtown. Next to our motel, we saw a sign at the Ellis Island Casino, which reads, "24 Hour Fine Dining," At 2:30 a.m., on both mornings, we had ham and eggs for $1.59. The sign should read, "24 Hour Cheap Dining."

Highlight of the trip--four of us handed a risky $125 each to scalpers to get into the Elton John/Billy Joel concert. It was Elton's birthday. Four hours of the finest entertainment I've ever seen. A sold out MGM Grand Garden Arena on a Saturday night is insane. Some of America's most beautiful women are on display. Young ones hanging on to old codgers wearing cowboy hats and gold chains, holding fat wads of bills. Bruce offered a beer to an Oriental beauty sitting in front of us. She turned him down. Then we realized that she was about 15 years-old, and with her parents.

The week-end wasn't cheap. I blew about the same amount of money I spent on dating in Orange County last month. But the trip was more fun than the dating.

Las Vegas is nuts. Every craps table full, $100 bills dropping like confetti. Where does all of that money come from? Most of it just goes down a slot and disappears. It's not a place to meet women. I suppose it could be if one worked at it, but there's too much else to do, and too many con artists around.

On the way back, we stopped at Stateline again. In the van there was women talk, gambling talk, and trash talk. Then the rear seats fell silent. The boys were sound asleep. I was at the wheel again, facing a six-hour drive home.

We never saw the 20 year-olds from Norco.

# Reader Comments and Tom's Responses

Florence: "You guys acted like a bunch of teen-age jerks!"
Response: *But gosh we had fun.*

Elaine: "Drinking and driving takes the cake for stupidity."
Response: *You are right. At least the driver did not drink. Having an open container in a vehicle is against the law. We were foolish.*

Marilyn: "Your Las Vegas column was the best ever. It captured grown men having some fun, letting their hair down, without getting too crazy. Next year, my husband wants to go along."
Response: *Sometime, we all need to get away. I can still taste those eggs we ate at 2 a.m. Have your husband call us.*

Al: "Considering the level of woman you've been describing lately, maybe you should change the name of the column to "Dog Date Afternoon." Response: *Not a bad idea. I've had some dog dates lately, haven't I.*

## COLUMN 46

# THE BROWN BAG DIAMOND AFFAIR

They met line-dancing at the Country Rock Cafe in Lake Forest. He's 49. She's 46. Her home is within walking distance of the dance hall. Romance bloomed for 15 weeks.

They discussed living together. He would rent his Mission Viejo home and move in with her. He'd pay her mortgage. She, the utilities and household expenses, including food. His share of the arrangement would cost considerably more.

They enjoyed bike riding together. She said: "You deserve a new 10-speed. Let's go shopping." It was nice to finally have a woman putting him first, even though it would be his money they'd be spending. He didn't know, but near the bike shop was a jewelry store at which she had pre-selected a $7000 engagement ring with the jeweler. After bike shopping, she innocently asked: "Can we stop in here?" The jeweler told them straight-faced that if they bought that day, they could get a $800 month-of-March discount.

An unexpected $7327 was added to the Visa card he had just used to purchase his new bike. His head was spinning. He had been taken by surprise. He rationalized that he had made her happy and he was merely investing in his future with her.

For three days he smoldered, displeased with the diamond. They needed the money for more practical things. And didn't men usually initiate ring decisions? Her act caused him to think about the mortgage payment. His ex-wife said, "Charlie, you're getting screwed."

He left a message on his fiancee's machine, "Dolly, let's chat about the mortgage payment." Sensing a problem, she called back, "How's my country-bunkin' doing?" He revised his offer, "Let's split *all* living expenses."

She responded, "You know that I have my elderly mother to support. Are you afraid of losing your aerospace job? Do you have doubts about us? Are you insecure?" A litany of demeaning questions flowed from her mouth. He couldn't believe his ears. Then she delivered a knockout punch, "I can't live with your revised proposal. Do you want the ring back?"

He asked, "Can't we discuss this over a cowboy cha-cha tomorrow?" She said, "No. And furthermore, I'm leaving the ring on my front porch. If you want to pick it up, that's your business." He knew she was only kidding.

A couple of hours later, he casually stopped by her house. There, in plain sight, for all the world to see and for anybody to take, was a brown paper bag with the $7000 diamond inside. He was glad he hadn't waited all day to pick it up. To him, the relationship was over.

Ten days later, she left a message, "I miss you terribly. My friends said I made a major mistake. May we go dancing Wednesday and discuss our feelings?" He agreed.

Ridin' Double, Black Velvet, all the dances. It was like old times. She whispered, "I love you," and was a clinging vine all night. "We can split the mortgage and other expenses," she whispered in his ear. She had gathered herself. The relationship was being salvaged. He was a happy two-stepper.

Over a kiss in his car, she asked, "Where are you safekeeping the ring?" He said, "I wanted to talk to you about the ring incident. I was upset." She responded, "I understand. When the time is right, we'll select a more practical ring. But you still have it, don't you?"

"No," he replied. She went icy cold and said, "Well, that changes things, doesn't it?" He replied, "I don't see why it should. We'll discuss it when we go dancing this week-end."

Early Saturday, she called, "I have no feelings for you..." "Whoa," he cut her off. Then, he was reminded of a line from a 1974 Joan Baez song, "Diamonds and Rust," something about not wanting to go through the diamond thing all over again. He had had enough. He had already paid.

They haven't talked since. The jeweler refunded his money. Time for a bike ride and a new dance partner.

## Reader Comments and Tom's Responses

Gene: "Regarding your column about the diamond ring: I'm 49, and have been on my own since September. Maybe for men, being single isn't so bad. Who wants to go through that kind of stuff? He was lucky it didn't work. She wasn't in love. She cared more about what her friends thought and the size of the ring on her finger." Response: *Imagine, her leaving that ring on her front porch in a paper bag.*

Jackie: "Someday, tell us about your favorite lady." Response: *How about today? Her name is Kira. She's my 12-year-old St. Bernard-Shepard mix. She might have left a paper bag on the front porch with something in it, but it wouldn't have been a diamond ring.*

## COLUMN 47

# A CONCERT BY THE SEA
# IN SAN DIEGO

It was one of those nights where you don't know what to expect. Not from your date, but from the events planned for the evening. A woman friend and I drove to San Diego on a Tuesday to see a singer we'd never heard of at a place we'd never been.

Our hosts, 30-year friends Terry and Billie, were also unfamiliar with the performer. They knew I liked country and western music and that's what Neil McCoy plays.

Humphrey's Half Moon Inn on Shelter Island in San Diego hosts a summer concert series. The venue is small, a perfect place to view a concert. About 2000 folding chairs on grass face the stage, not a bad seat anywhere. Off to the left rest a myriad of yachts. Across the water, million dollar homes dot the hillside.

We weren't sitting on the lawn. A hotel room had been rented which overlooks the chairs and offers an unobstructed view of the stage.

Joining us were my sister, Pam, and her husband, Bob. For them, an emotional night. Bob was leaving two days later for a six month tour of duty as a ship captain.

The popping of a champagne cork signaled the start of the picnic. George Killian's Irish Red Lager and Arizona Teas were iced in the cooler. Banana peppers filled with cream cheese puckered lips. Chicken salad sandwiches, Hav-a-Chips, deviled eggs, and pasta salad filled empty stomachs. When the band took the stage, we didn't know what to expect. If we didn't like the music, it wouldn't matter. We could just slip inside the suite and enjoy old friends' company.

But Neil McCoy is a sensational country performer. Before long, he had the six middle agers bouncing and jiving on the balcony. My sister and hubby have been married 22 years. They were dancing like teenagers. A night of unknown expectation turned out to be special.

The next morning, we had breakfast on the deck at the Red Sails Inn overlooking the boats. Two mallard ducks strolled among the tables, pecking at shoelaces, demanding eggs benedict.

Then the most unexpected thrill of our short trip: America's Cup stuff. We paid $20 to enter the New Zealand compound for a close look at racing boat *Black Magic I*. The sleek beauty was in dry-dock, resting like a proud Kiwi, one victory away from a Cup sweep. In four months of sailing, with a record of 41-1, she's the fastest in the world.

Reality arrived at noon. I was back in Dana Point working at my deli and my date had an afternoon meeting. The Humphrey's concert series runs well into the fall. Performers like Chuck Berry, Little Richard, and Bill Cosby are scheduled. We'll go back.

An hour's drive from South County, Humphrey's is a unique place to go with a date. And you never know what to expect when old friends get together.

## Reader Comments and Tom's Responses

Pooh: "You sure get around. The concert sounded fun."
Response: *There are lots of opportunities in Southern California. You just have to seek them out.*

Sally: "All of this country and western stuff you write about is a bore. Why don't you try the symphony and other more culturally-preferred events? Then, I might consider going out with you."
Response: *Doubt if you and I would do well together. Sounds like you're a little too stiff and up there in the clouds for me. Can I wear shorts and tennis shoes with a tuxedo?*

Jake: "Thanks for the tip on Humphrey's. I'm going to check out Bill Cosby." Response: *You mean as a date or a performer? I think Bill's married. At least on television he is.*

## COLUMN 48

# A LETTER TO JIMMY LEFERE

Last week, I received a letter from Jimmy Lefere. We grew up together in Jackson, Michigan. He still lives there. We haven't seen each other since 1957. Two years ago, we exchanged letters. This is my current response:

"Dear Jimmy:

A few things have changed in the two years since we wrote each other. On Xmas Eve, '93, my wife backed up a U-haul to our home, took what she wanted, and left. The only hitch--I didn't know about it. I was visiting Mom in Northern California. She never came back.

So, 1994 was an adjustment year. In *Graceland*, Paul Simon sings about a woman in New York City who feels like a human trampoline. I relate to how she feels, bouncing all over the place. The divorce was final March 24th. This is the third time I've divided my assets in this manner. It's amazing there's anything left.

Anyway, out of adversity comes opportunity. Or something like that. I started keeping notes about my separation and subsequent re-entry into the dating world. I wrote a 4-part short story to myself over a four month period. The material looked pretty good so I shopped around to see if anyone would be interested in publishing it.

Last July, *The Orange County Register* started my column entitled, "Middle Aged and Dating," in seven South Orange

County weekly newspapers it owns. The readership of the weeklies is estimated at 140,000. So far, **48** columns have run. There's a large following because there are so many middle aged singles out there trying to make some sense of life. At 55, having blind dates, getting dumped, rejected, or fired. Struggling to make mortgage payments, that sort of thing. When you and I hunted for bullfrogs in 1945, life was less complicated.

Is middle aged dating any different in the Midwest? Or is it just Californians who tend to screw up everything?

Recently, I wrote a column about a visit by my high school sweetie. You probably knew her. She's a single in Washington, D.C. now, and not exactly having a picnic on the White House lawn.

My deli's doing great. I run my dog a couple of miles a day. I 've been dating a special widow for 7 months. After 18 years of marriage, she's still dealing with her loss. Since my separation, I've had dates with **33** different women. Gives one an idea of how hard it is to find someone with whom one's compatible. Going out has provided lots of info for a book I'm writing. After people read that, there probably will be an increase in church attendance nationwide, or at least in Orange County.

Never thought my life would be this way at 55. But, I'm healthy and nothing else really matters. Would be nice to see you one of these years.

Tom"

## Reader Comments and Tom's Responses

Chuck: "In 17 months, you've dated 33 women. In 19 months, I haven't even met 33 women. Guess I should get a deli." Response: *Why don't you just borrow or rent mine?*

Shirley: "The letter you wrote to your friend was very moving. I was the fourth wife of my late husband. He was the greatest thing that ever happened to me. We had a wonderful marriage. Fourth is the best. Bless you." Response: *A fourth wife? Me? My pockets aren't deep enough.*

Anne: "Wake up and smell the coffee, 55 is not middle aged. You're entering the golden years." Response: *With gusto baby.*

## COLUMN 49

# TOM IS GOING TO STOP DATING

After 17 months of being single, I've decided to stop dating. I've had a truckload of dates--been out probably 250 times. Never counted. There have been hangovers, hang ups and hangers on. Some readers suggest I try too hard. They are probably right.

Two relationships mattered this time. One was stormy. I gave it a shot, but got tired of taking boxing gloves on our dates. My nickname for her was Captain Combat at first, Captain Nasty later. I'm not a fighter but was with her.

The second relationship, frankly, I wanted to work. Eight months were invested. During that time, there were gaps when we weren't together. But we never let each other get far away. Guess we cared a lot. It seems the relationship had fewer problems in the beginning than toward the end. Maybe it was because we got to know each other better and weren't comfortable.

There were plenty of relationship incompatibility warning signs. Sometimes we put blinders on because our hearts are so involved.

She felt because I never had children, I couldn't adjust to hers and the grandchildren. Hogwash. Just because a person never had kids doesn't mean they don't like them. Women who pontificate about men who never had kids irritate the hell out of me. Like there's something wrong with us. As if, now, at age 55, we can change our past and make as if we had kids.

Maybe too many of her pals told her not to date that Casanova guy who writes this dating column. That's sad, I'm not much different than the rest of the folks out there trying. I just write about dating in seven newspapers and maybe work a little harder at it than most. If I ever settle down, I will continue to write about dating, but other people will become the subject.

Whatever, I've busted my tail trying to make it work. She did too. As best she could. I got tired of hearing what she thought *I* need in a woman. When a woman starts talking like that, beware. When a relationship is too out of balance, the one receiving the short end of the stick needs to move on.

So, why stop dating? It's just too tiring, too much work. All I want is to love and appreciate someone and them me. It seems too hard to find a woman who fills that bill. Also, I realize I carry my share of old baggage around.

Dating is also too expensive. Forty dollars here, fifty bucks there. One can easily spend $1000 a month without too much effort. Who's got that kind of money lying around?

Also, dating takes too much time. Imagine if the time spent so far had been invested in more productive pursuits. I could have rewritten the Dead Sea Scrolls by now.

When you think about it, dating is a lot like golf. It takes too much time, is too expensive and frustrating, and doesn't provide much exercise. Once in a while you get a hole in one or make a nice shot which keeps you going. I don't play golf very well either.

Others I know have thrown in the dating towel. They say they're happier. Perhaps. I'm not convinced.

What will happen to this column? I'll write about other people's adventures. Then, readers can throw darts at them.

So, it's time to regroup. To stay home. To learn to be happy by myself. To work on personal goals. Maybe I'll take a trip with the money saved. I hope this seven day hiatus from dating isn't too hard on me.

## Reader Comments and Tom's Responses

Anita: "What a riot. You really had us scared that you were going to stop dating altogether. The week off will do you good." Response: *Yea. I hope I can stand it, but I'm already experiencing hot flashes.*

Anonymous Woman: "For you, a seven day break from dating isn't long enough." Response: *If anything, it was too long.*

Lana: "Trying too hard doesn't get one anywhere. Men can put themselves out there like peacocks but women make the choices. You can't tell if a relationship will work until you try. Take a break. The right one might show up." Response: *I think your message is to just ease up. I agree.*

Shirley: "Regarding potential wife number four. If you find the right woman, you won't need deep pockets." Response: *Where is she? Where is she?*

## COLUMN 50

# A YEAR OF MIDDLE AGE DATING COLUMNS

When this column began last July, I had no idea how many I'd get to write. Assistant Managing Editor Dixie Redfearn said if I provided her with four acceptable columns, she would give me a shot. She also mumbled, "I hope you appreciate this opportunity. We get requests from about 1000 people a year to write columns."

I do appreciate this opportunity. To write, to be published, and read-- I'm a lucky man. Neither life nor this column is taken for granted.

Here we are, column #50, a year's worth. Was there a favorite? All of them. Labors of love. Lesson learned: Keep plugging daily.

Early on, there was a danger of running out of women to date. So I secretly checked out the ladies at the newspaper. Dixie's happily married so she was out. Editor Sherrie was single but moved on to *The Register,* or the big paper as I like to call it. Jo was closer to my age, but left on vacation for Colorado the week I wanted to ask her. Business manager Marilyn just knows too many people and could make it tough on me in social circles.

That left my editor, Susan. What do you think she meant when I hinted once about meeting for coffee? "Not in your very wildest of dreams." I was relieved. Our philosophies are very different.

Hence, I had to scour the streets of Orange County, California, looking for dates. The International House of Pancakes near Leisure World was a good place. And just down Rockfield, so was c & w dance hall, The Country Rock Cafe. The Cowboy Boogie Club in Anaheim is too long of a drive--that 32 mile trip home late at night is a drag.

The Dana Point Resort, where we hold our singles functions, was productive. As were Hennessey's and the Ocean Avenue Brewery in Laguna Beach.

The Ritz Carlton Hotel is a singles paradise if you don't mind drinking alone. Prego, a restaurant in Irvine, cost me $88, and the date only lasted three hours.

The Swallows Inn in San Juan Capistrano has some pretty tough characters hanging out there. Harpoon Henry's in the harbor is a good place to meet. But for me, the best place: my deli in Dana Point.

Besides Mom, is there a special woman yet? Not in the true sense of the word. She knows who she is. So do most readers of this column. I once compared her to a confused airplane, circling, trying to decide where to land. Maybe in '95 she will. Perhaps she won't. Relationships don't blossom if both sides aren't ready.

Dating has exposed me to culture. How else would I have learned who Charles Wysocki is? Contrary to one friend's opinion, his work is not like a Motel 6 lobby art show.

There were concerts by my friend of 20 years, Johnny Cash, and Neil McCoy, Alan Jackson, Billy Joel and Elton John.

Overall, not a bad year. I've had better and worse. Am I more mature and less confused? A little. Will I keep dating? Yes. At a slower pace. As time goes on, the urgency "to be out there all of the time" diminishes.

To my readers, thanks for your support, barbs, daggers, opinions, and love. Each of you is an individual. Each important, each special. That I have learned.

## Reader Comments and Tom's Responses

Lana: "You are a kind and caring man, able to communicate your feelings which is rare for a man. Why can't readers just ask questions instead of passing judgments on you?" Response: *Thanks. I needed that. Kinda been getting pounded pretty hard lately.*

Jo: "Why don't you publish a book on dating?" Response: *I plan to, maybe as many as three volumes. The first one is going to be called, "Middle Aged and Dating Again," which is an acronym for MAD again. There is a little of that in this business also.*

To order additional copies of **Middle Aged and Dating Again**, complete the information below.

Ship to: (please print)

Name_____

Address_____

City, State, Zip_____

Day phone_____

_____ copies of *Middle Aged and Dating Again* @ $12.95 each $ _____

Postage and handling @ $2.50 per book $ _____

California residents add 7.75 % tax $ _____

Total amount enclosed $ _____

*Make checks payable to Middle Aged and Dating Again*

**Send to:  15 Reina**
**Dana Point, CA 92629 • 714-248-8219**

------------------------------------------------------------

To order additional copies of **Middle Aged and Dating Again**, complete the information below.

Ship to: (please print)

Name_____

Address_____

City, State, Zip_____

Day phone_____

_____ copies of *Middle Aged and Dating Again* @ $12.95 each $ _____

Postage and handling @ $2.50 per book $ _____

California residents add 7.75 % tax $ _____

Total amount enclosed $ _____

*Make checks payable to Middle Aged and Dating Again*

**Send to:  15 Reina**
**Dana Point, CA 92629 • 714-248-8219**